You Send Me

Jan. 2023

Also by Patricia T. O'Conner

*Woe Is I: The Grammarphobe's Guide to
Better English in Plain English*

*Words Fail Me: What Everyone Who Writes
Should Know About Writing*

You Send Me

*Getting It Right
When You Write Online*

Patricia T. O'Conner

and

Stewart Kellerman

A Harvest Book
Harcourt, Inc.
Orlando   Austin   New York   San Diego   Toronto   London

Copyright © 2002 by Patricia T. O'Conner and Stewart Kellerman

www.HarcourtBooks.com

Library of Congress Cataloging-in-Publication Data
O'Conner, Patricia T.
You send me: getting it right when you write online/
Patricia T. O'Conner and Stewart Kellerman.—1st ed.
p.   cm.
Includes bibliographical references and index.
ISBN 0-15-100593-1   ISBN 0-15-602733-X (pbk.)
1. English language—Rhetoric—Data processing.   2. Electronic mail
messages—Authorship.   3. Report writing—Data processing.
4. Online data processing.   I. Kellerman, Stewart.   II. Title.
PE1408.O36 2002
808'.042'0285—dc21   2001006287

Designed by Linda Lockowitz
Text set in Adobe Garamond
First Harvest edition 2003
K J I H G F E D C B A

Printed in the United States of America

For Jane Isay

Contents

Acknowledgments   xi

Introduction   1

PART I   The Virtual Mensch

1. Protocool
Attitude Adjustment   9

2. All's Well That Sends Well
Anatomy of an E-Mail   29

3. To E or Not to E
When Online's Out of Line   46

4. Accustomed to Your Interface
Keeping the Reader in Mind   63

5. A Click and a Promise
Getting the Facts Straight   81

PART II   Alpha Mail

6. Natural Selection
Conciser Is Nicer   95

7. The E-Mail Eunuch
Beefing Up Wussy Writing   105

8. The Trite Stuff
Nipping Clichés in the Bud   121

9. Wired Write
Are You Making Sense?   129

10. Get a Virtual Life
Operating Instructions   140

PART III   Words of Passage

11. Grammar à la Modem
A Crash Course   149

12. Go Configure
Abused, Confused, and Misused Words   172

13. Alphabet Soup
Spelling It Right   182

14. Period Piece
The Perils of Punctuation   201

Afterword   225
Bibliography   227
Index   231

Acknowledgments

A good editor is a reader's best friend (as we never tired of saying back when we were editors ourselves). *You Send Me* was the inspiration of our editor, Jane Isay, whose taste, good sense, and unerring eye as a reader have been a source of amazement, year after year and book after book. They don't make editors like Jane anymore, or agents like Dan Green, either. We're very fortunate to have the two of them on our side.

Anyone who doubts that wired people can be literate should meet the folks in our electronic address book, which we've shamelessly plundered in gathering material. Scores of friends and colleagues generously shared their e-mail experiences and their perspectives of life online, and the debt we owe them is evident on every page. Giga-thanks to Avi Arditti, Laurie Asséo, Eva Barczay, Brenda Berkman, André Bernard, Bruce Brassfield, Michelle Brook, Wendy Carlos, Jo Ellyn Clarey, Isabel Cymerman, Charles

Doherty, Laurel E. Doherty, Rachel Elkind-Tourre, David Feldman, Rob Franciosi, Elizabeth Frenchman, Bryan A. Garner, Anita Gates, Millie Goldberg, Jane Green, Jeannine Green, Simon Green, James Harris, David Hawkins, Dan Jacob, Nancy Jacob, Dimitra Karras, Nicholas Karras, Niki Karras, Panayota Karras, Peter Keepnews, Ann Kirschner, Harvey Kleinman, Jean Kummerow, Michael J. Leahy, Eden Ross Lipson, Stephen Miller, Margaret Miner, Deborah Nye, Sophie Nye, Virginia Parker, Merrill Perlman, Jeanne Pinder, David Rampe, Haylee Richard, Simon Rodberg, Brian Rose, Steven Schwartz, Michael Sniffen, Marilyn Stasio, Gloria Gardiner Urban, Bruce Washburn, Liz Weis, Marilynn K. Yee, and Kate Murphy Zeman.

For service above and beyond the call of duty, our heartfelt gratitude to Jude Biersdorfer, who was kind enough to read the manuscript. Her technical expertise saved us many sleepless nights and several embarrassments, while her humor and insights had a way of making old terrain fresh again. And if medical science ever succeeds in cloning a human being, the first subject should be Anna Jardine. The world could use more copy editors like her.

We're indebted to the readers of *Woe Is I* and *Words Fail Me,* whose cards and letters are a constant reminder that English is a many-splendored thing. Thanks, too, to Leonard Lopate of WNYC radio and to the faithful and perspicacious listeners of "New York and Company."

Our families, wired and non-, have been steady sources of support, encouragement, and ideas. We owe much to Beverly Newman, Kathy Richard, and Allen, Craig, Larry, and Pamela Kellerman.

Thank you, one and all. We promise never to send you chain letters, forward indiscriminately, share your e-mail addresses without permission, or take three screenfuls to get to the point.

You Send Me

Introduction

There was a mini-crisis in our family a while ago when Pat's mom, in a fit of housecleaning zeal, sold an old cookie jar, a simple brown and white ceramic cow, at a garage sale for fifty cents. Pat's sister called us, nearly in tears. She'd loved that cow since it was Grandma's, and she took the loss hard.

"Don't worry, we'll find you another," we told her. How hard could it be to find a cow cookie jar? We'd stop at an antique shop or a flea market and pick one up for her birthday.

Several weeks and eleven flea markets later, we admitted defeat. There were lots of cookie jars, but no cows. Or not the *right* cow. We needed your basic Bossie, not one wearing a tutu and definitely not a bull in top hat and tux, smoking a cigar.

Just when we'd about decided to settle for a tasteful pig, Stewart thought of the Internet. Of course! We searched the Web under "cookie jar."

You can probably guess what happened next. We stumbled into a bizarre parallel universe, an alien culture inhabited by collectors and dealers and hobbyists and nostalgia buffs for whom the cookie jar has little to do with cookies. We found Humpty-Dumpty cookie jars, Mr. Peanut cookie jars, celebrity cookie jars both old and new, rare and common. There were cookie jars shaped like trolls and monks, fire engines, Santa Clauses, tractors, American presidents, British prime ministers, and every insect and amphibian and mammal known to taxonomy, including cows.

Before long, we were trading e-mails with a woman in Ohio who bought and sold cookie jars for a living and had at least half a dozen that fit our description. A few days later, our selection arrived by snail mail, a standard 1950's Elsie-type cow, not in the least rare but in perfect condition and bubble-wrapped to a fare-thee-well. It cost around $30. We were elated, although by that time Pat's sister had forgotten about the whole thing.

Most of the people we know have stories like this—not necessarily about their mothers' selling stuff at garage sales, but about how the computer has insinuated itself into their lives. Jeannine, an executive for a multinational company, runs projects with tentacles in the United States, Europe, and the Far East. She used to stay up all hours trying to juggle clients in three or four time zones. She had no life— until she started using e-mail instead of the phone.

Now she can do her work and catch some Z's, too. Nancy, a retired high school English teacher, had the opposite problem. She suffers from insomnia and used to tiptoe around the house till dawn with nothing to do. Now she can boot up, go online, and "talk" to her friends in the wee hours without disturbing them.

What's remarkable about these stories is how unremarkable they are. Thanks to the Internet, people are finding not only cows and jobs and places to live and cures for hives and recipes for goulash and new ways to do business. They're finding each other, connecting with a client here, a distant cousin there, a new dermatologist, an old roommate, an ad manager, an ex-coach.

And they're doing it in writing. The big cheese who wouldn't have been caught dead touching a typewriter in pre-digital times can't survive these days without a laptop and e-mail. The college student who used to call home when the well ran dry now posts a message to Mom's Web site. The middle schooler who once gossiped on the phone all evening ties up the line swapping instant messages. Can you believe it? Writing is cool again.

Well, virtual writing. The truth is that much of what passes for writing in cyberspace is dreadful. The spelling in e-mail is rotten, the grammar is atrocious, the punctuation—don't ask. And e-mail isn't the half of it. Some of the drivel in chat rooms and instant messages, on bulletin boards and Web pages doesn't deserve to be called writing. No wonder people who love language are wringing their hands and saying the computer has been a disaster for the written word.

Now back up just a nanosecond. We love language, too, but we think the computer may turn out to be the best thing that's happened to writing since the printing press.

True, your typical e-mail is not a pretty sight. No doubt the speed, the breeziness, the spontaneity, the directness of online writing—precisely what people like so much about it—contribute to its sloppiness. But don't blame the computer for the rotten state of writing. If anything, we should thank it for exposing the problem and making writing an essential skill again. The real reason writing is so bad in cyberspace is that people simply don't write well anymore, online or off.

If you want to blame technology, blame the telephone. People with even a few years of grade school used to be competent writers. Then the phone came along and made the art of letter writing optional. As if that weren't enough, society began pooh-poohing "proper" English—grammar, spelling, composition—and school after school stopped teaching it in the late 1960's and early 70's.

But enough finger-pointing. What's important is that we're writing again, and it's better to write badly than not at all. If our writing needs work, we can do something about it. Writing is a skill like any other.

"Writing?" you say. "But I'm not a writer."

Hello? Not a writer? What's that you're doing every day in front of your computer screen?

Though writing in the virtual world isn't exactly like writing in the real one, it's writing all the same. Technology may change by the hour, but no matter how often you upgrade your word-processing program, you're still processing words. And putting together a good e-mail is a lot easier than installing a new word processor, at least for two computer semiliterates like us. What matters is that it works.

People who still ask whether online writing has to be good writing just don't get it. Words, whether etched in stone, written in sand, sent by Morse code, inked on parchment, or transmitted in bytes, serve only one purpose: to connect us with other people. When you write well, you connect. When you write badly, you don't.

Take e-mail, for example. What kind of connection is it? Shall we treat it as formal writing? Or as casual speech? Or is it something in the middle? Most of the people we ask think it falls somewhere between a letter and a phone call. Not surprisingly, those who think e-mail is closer to letter-writing are pickier about spelling and grammar and such. Those who think it's closer to speech are more forgiving about things like typos and "creative" punctuation.

Yet both sides agree that online writing could use a few rules, even if they disagree about when to call in the grammar police. In fact, standards are already evolving. You help set them every time you sit down at your keyboard. A trendy lawyer who writes "kewl" and "L8R" instead of "cool" and "later" won't keep it up if her clients stumble over the shorthand or find it obnoxious. A well-meaning CPA won't go on sending everybody in the office the same long strings of jokes if twelve co-workers ask to be taken off his mailing list. And the kid who never spell-checks will learn his lesson when he tries to order tickets to an Eminem concert and ends up in the front row at Mostly Mozart.

Right now online writing is pretty much in its Wild West stage, a free-for-all with everybody shooting from the hip and no sheriff in sight. The outlaws claim that rules are so *analog,* so *print,* so *old media.* But law and order will gradually replace frontier justice, and now is our chance to have a say in what the laws will be.

PART I

The Virtual Mensch

1. Protocool
Attitude Adjustment

Our friend Miles loves his job in the entertainment industry, but he dreads opening his e-mail. He never knows what will jump out of his in-box and grab him by the throat. Messages between colleagues have become curt, rude, aggressive. Sentences are often mere commands, shortened to quick barks. There's a sense that to be nice in e-mail is to show weakness. It's gotten so bad that Miles is seeing a cognitive therapist to help him deal with the stress.

Welcome to the dark side. Sure, the digital revolution is awesome, the niftiest thing to come along since the wheel. Computers have made writing routine for people who almost never wrote before. Online bulletin boards, chat rooms, instant messages, Web pages, newsgroups, and the like have brought new meaning to the word "community." And e-mail has single-handedly revived the epistolary tradition, the venerable practice of writing letters.

But not everybody's cheering. Miles (he asked us not to use his real name) isn't the only one who finds this new world hard to take. Others grumble about spam assaults, wacko chain letters, waves of mass-forwarded jokes, in-your-face instant messages, Web sites to nowhere, boorish behavior in chat rooms, complicated downloads that tie up their computers, and rampant misinformation. Some people are so bummed by e-mail that they won't have anything to do with it. So there!

It's not hard to see what's happening. Like kids on their first visit to Toys "Я" Us, we're experimenting with these new ways to communicate, trying to fit a square peg into a round hole or make a dump truck fly or see through the wrong end of a telescope. If we want to play nicely with others, boys and girls, we'll have to learn how to use our new toys.

The Mouse That Roared

A corporate president we know showed us an e-mail that a software developer had sent to her and a dozen other people in her company. The message announced plans for a training session and added: "Please let me know if you would be interested in attending or if you would like an underling to attend."

Ouch! Let's hope the training session wasn't about sensitivity in the workplace.

It's strange how online writing can bring out the tactless oaf in even the nicest person. The dunderhead who sent that e-mail would never have used the word "underling" in a memo to be tacked up on the office bulletin board. Yet there it was, dropped as casually as you please into a mailing to a long list of people. Why not use the PA system?

The next time you e-mail, show a little tact. For starters, adjust your attitude before you begin writing. Imagine how your message will look to the reader, and write the kind of e-mail you'd like to get if the tables were turned. When you've finished, reread the message before letting it go. Look for dissonant notes (like "underling"). As Jane, our editor, often says, "Leave no tone unturned." And never, never, *never* hit Send in anger—hit Send Later and store the radioactive material until you've cooled off.

Why bother being nice? Because it's too easy to be misunderstood when you're writing modem à modem. Let us count the ways: What's convenient shorthand for you may seem cold and abrupt, even nasty, to the reader. Small slights are magnified. A tiny, half-joking pout can look like a major hissy fit. The mildest of suggestions may sound like a rebuke. Subtlety, irony, and sarcasm can land with a thud. And in mass mailings, now an important part of office life, the chances for misunderstanding are multiplied by the number of readers.

Certainly, the computer has brought us closer together. But it's also turned us into a scrappy, suspicious bunch and made cyberspace a quarrelsome place.

The plain truth is that connecting sometimes drives people apart. Virtual behavior is often bad behavior, perhaps because the speed and the anonymity of on-line writing give messages a hard edge. Is it any surprise that something written in a clipped, telegraphed manner comes across as gruff and snippy?

The very structure of e-mail encourages curtness. The blank subject line staring you in the face is a signal to state your business and get on with it, and almost precludes a warm message. The To and From fields seem to make salutations and greetings and signatures redundant or unnecessary. What we have here is the ideal breeding ground for rudeness.

Once upon a time, a huffy or overwrought letter-writer had a built-in cooling-off period—the time it took to address an envelope, find a stamp, and get to a mailbox. She could always change her mind along the way and tear up that nuclear missive. Chances are, you too have written letters that for one reason or another were never mailed.

But how many unwise e-mails have you intercepted in time? Almost everyone has regrets. One exec we know blew up when a pet item was vetoed from the company budget. The angry message, lamented for years afterward: "Fine, then take it out of my salary!" And you probably read about the CEO in Kansas City who made headlines when an overheated e-mail of his was leaked to a Yahoo message board and took on a life of its own. The company's stock plunged and he was forced to apologize.

What he needed was a tact-checker. Actually, the e-mail program Eudora has one, a feature called MoodWatch that's supposed to warn you when you're about to say something better left unsaid. Regrettably, the reviews haven't been good. A computer can help you think, but it can't think for you. So use your own judgment and watch your own mood.

Mail Bonding

We shudder to think what Dale Carnegie would make of cyberspace. Some wired types seem determined to lose friends and alienate people. Apparently manners aren't evolving as fast as technology, so it's cold out there. If you want to take the chill off, try doing these warm-up exercises next time you log on.

- Reacquaint yourself with a few quaint English words, like "please," "thanks," and "sorry." Why abandon the pleasantries merely because you're online? If you need something, ask—don't demand. Show your appreciation when someone's been helpful. And apologize when you step on toes.
- Go the extra word. Online writing doesn't have to be abrupt. You're not paying by the word; why sound like a classified ad?
- Be forgiving. Don't let an ill-mannered e-mail set

you off. You didn't mean to be a horse's patoot when you went online, and the person who messaged you probably didn't either. Give him the benefit of the doubt.

- Use some of the courtesies of letter writing. A friendly greeting, a polite closing, and a name at the end can do plenty to thaw out a cold message.
- Be patient. Don't expect an immediate reply, especially when your message is unsolicited. If it's really a matter of life or death, don't e-mail—call 911.
- Set the right tone. It's better to sound too nice than not nice enough. Take out any word that might be hurtful, and stick in any that might warm up your message. We're not crazy about smiley-face symbols or cute abbreviations or bracketed asides (there's more about them in chapter 4), but if they'll help prevent a misunderstanding, then why not? Free-spirited doesn't have to be mean-spirited.

Before you can do all this, you'll need to grow a new set of antennae. Many of the old assumptions about behavior no longer compute. The world, particularly the world of work, isn't what it used to be. Technology has changed our jobs and has even affected how we look and dress and talk. In some offices, every day is casual Friday and five-o'clock shadow is considered sexy. In others, pets come to work and kids go to day care down the hall. Flex time, job sharing, telecommuting, and home offices have turned the workday upside down.

Manners, too, will have to evolve. You can't say the same thing in an e-mail, for example, that you'd say in person. Imagine you're a supervisor and you want to gently prod an employee. If you happen to be passing by his cubicle, you might poke your head in, give him a big smile and a thumbs-up, and say, "So? Where is it? The clock is ticking!" But if the guy works from home or in a distant office, an e-mail bluntly delivering the identical message—"So? Where is it? The clock is ticking!"—might scare the pants off him.

People expect to be treated like human beings, even online. So remember to do your warm-up exercises.

Post Haste

Looking at our electronic in-basket, we sometimes feel like the Red Queen in *Through the Looking-Glass.* It takes all the running we can do to stay in the same place.

A few messages always sit around longer than we'd like, but we try to clear up the important ones as soon as they come in. If we can't reply to an e-mail right away—maybe it requires some digging—we'll usually send a short message saying we're on the case.

We work at home, so our business and personal lives overlap, especially in our in-basket. But even the commuter crowd gets at least some personal e-mail at work, never mind the rules. Some people use the same in-box for business and personal mail, as we do. Others have personal messages sent to a special folder; what's left in the folder at the end of the work-day can be forwarded to their home computers. Hey, whatever works.

There are e-mail programs that let you sort your messages by time, size, subject, sender, and so on, but don't depend on software to manage your mailbox for you. Stewart once bought a big old roll-top desk to bring order to his life, but what he ended up with was a messy roll-top desk. You'll have to organize your mind, budget your time, and stick to whatever sys-tem works for you.

Some people use the first-in, first-out method; others answer the most important messages first and the least important last; and still others reply to the easiest first and save the hardest for later. We think of our in-box as a virtual emergency room. The critical cases are handled first. The broken arms come next. The colds and sniffles can wait.

The ER approach really works. You only need some discipline. It may be more fun to answer that long, leisurely e-mail from the college roommate you haven't seen for ten years. But control yourself. Send a quick note saying a longer answer is in the works. Then go back to the emergencies. And don't make excuses about how busy or popular you are. The busiest people seem to have the emptiest mailboxes at the end of the day, or so they claim.

Is it possible to answer an e-mail *too* quickly? A couple we know in Reston, Virginia, have had what Stewart calls a discussion, and Pat an argument, on this very subject.

Steve, an efficient sort of fellow, likes to answer e-mail instantly, but Eva thinks it's rude to click Reply too soon. It's an interesting issue. The immediacy of e-mail has made the etiquette a little strange. Just because you *can* reply quickly, should you?

Eva feels that Steve puts pressure on the guy who e-mails him by answering a message the moment it comes in. The e-mailer thinks he has to reply just as quickly to Steve's reply, and so on, until the two of them are messaging each other twenty times a day.

We've noticed this ping-pong effect too, but we don't believe it has anything to do with how fast you reply. The problem is the *way* you reply.

Here's how you can avoid a speedy return of service the next time you e-mail somebody simply to say howdy. Make it clear that you don't expect an immediate response, maybe by saying, "Take your time answering" or "No need to reply." And don't, just to be sociable, toss in an offhand remark that requires an answer ("How old is the basset hound now?" or "Where'd you get those chipmunk suspenders?").

You also might consider waiting awhile before

messaging someone if all you have to say is hello. As
Simon, a Yale student, e-mailed us, "Keeping in touch
means saying something substantive, not merely
dropping a line." Now that's substantive.

Subject Matter

People would do a better job of answering e-mail
if they could tell at a glance which messages were important and which weren't. But not every important
e-mail comes from president@whitehouse.gov and
has the subject line "Wanna be a Supreme Court
Justice?"

Most of the subject lines that show up in our in-
basket are, to put it kindly, subjective. Anyone who's
ever tweaked a mouse knows what we're talking
about. The only way to tell whether a message is urgent or merely the joke du jour is to read it. With a
few dozen messages waiting to be read, where do you
begin?

There must be a better way. Actually, there is. But
it'll take the cooperation of the people who e-mail
you. And the best way to get it is to show some
yourself.

When you have something seismic to say, indicate
it in the subject line: *Flash! I'm quitting.* When you
don't, indicate that too: *Next year's vacation request.*
And when something can't wait, say so: *Need the spreadsheet now!* (But remember the boy who cried wolf.)

If you want your incoming mail to have helpful

subject lines, set a good outgoing example. (There's more on subject lines in chapter 2.)

Office Confidential

A few years after we left *The New York Times* to write full-time, the company fired almost two dozen employees at an accounting center in Virginia for sending "inappropriate and offensive" e-mail. Sound familiar?

Most people have sent an imprudent e-mail at one time or another. We plead guilty ourselves. If we were still at the *Times,* we'd be deleting a few things from our personal files, say that screen saver of Tom Cruise playing air guitar in his shorts or that shutdown sound of a flushing toilet.

The *Times* isn't the only company that tries to discourage employees from sending insensitive or off-color pictures, jokes, and remarks. Dow Chemical has fired scores of workers for sending inappropriate messages. And Xerox has canned scores more for surfing porn and shopping sites on the Web. The odds are that your company, too, has put in software to spy on employees' virtual activities. Most companies have, according to a survey by the American Management Association.

Is all this legit? Apparently so. The courts have ruled that employers can snoop to their hearts' content to make sure workers don't waste time, harass one another, steal company secrets, and so on.

So what should you do if you get the urge to act like a wise-ass at work? Don't even think about it. Take a deep breath or count to ten or lock yourself in the supply cabinet or crawl under your desk. Do whatever it takes, but never forget where you are and whose computer you're using.

Assume that someone with absolutely no sense of humor is hunched over a desktop computer in an office down the hall, monitoring every single thing you do online, from e-mailing your proctologist or your shrink to placing a bet at HialeahPark.com. If Bill Gates can't keep his e-mail private, neither can you.

No, it's not paranoia. Big Brother *is* watching. Or rather, he might be. And he's not necessarily your boss. What office doesn't have a busybody? Figure that someone—a temp in the Computer Department, a nosy parker in Accounting, perhaps the nerd in the next cubicle—is electronically looking over your shoulder whenever you go online.

You may trust the woman you're e-mailing, but what about the guy she forwards the message to? Or the propeller-head who cleans out the guy's hard drive when he quits to become a Hare Krishna? A three-year-old embarrassment that you thought was dead and buried may come back to haunt you. In short, don't put anything in an office e-mail that you wouldn't want the whole office to see. (Some companies archive all incoming and outgoing messages. Does yours?)

We're not talking only about embarrassing personal stuff. Confidential business messages are equally vulnerable to prying eyes. A lawyer friend advises clients not to e-mail anything sensitive, because his computer system isn't secure. Even if it were one hundred percent hacker-proof, the messages would still be subject to court orders and accessible by software like the FBI's e-mail snooping program, Carnivore.

You can relax a bit when you log on from home, but not too much. Software is out there that can track your every move, from the Web sites you visit to the books you buy to the songs you download to the e-mails you answer. Yes, there are programs that can foil casual snoopers; one of them is called PGP, for Pretty Good Privacy. But it's safer to operate on the assumption that virtually anyone can find out virtually anything you do in the virtual world. (Oh, and have a good night's sleep.)

That's especially true when you go public, say in a message to a newsgroup or bulletin board or Web page. God only knows who'll read it. If you could be embarrassed by something, don't say it online. Assume the bozo in Marketing with the plaid bow tie will read the wisecrack you post to alt.peeves about his taste in haberdashery. And be extra careful if your words might be libelous. We're thinking about the bonehead who thought an anonymous screen name would protect him when he claimed online that he'd had an affair with the CEO's wife. The chief executive hired a private eye, found out that the poster was an ex-employee, and took him to court.

Red Flags in the Workplace

Maybe you haven't heard of SuperScout, Message Inspector, TrafficMax, GameWarden, eSniff, or LittleBrother Pro, but they may have heard of you. Those are just a few of the programs a company can use to spy on employees when they're online. These are the kinds of things the software looks for:

- E-mail: Words or phrases that suggest harassment ("babe," "hooters," "talk dirty"); racism ("Aryan," "KKK," "white power"); job hunting ("curriculum vitae," "references," "signing bonus"); security breaches ("confidential," "eyes only," "secret," "proprietary"), going postal ("AK-47," "ammonium sulfate," "detonator," "pipe bomb," "unfair evaluation"); and vulgarity (oh, you know).

- Downloads: Those ".exe," ".zip," ".sit," and other files that indicate games, music, videos, and similar humongous attachments that hog disk space and overload computer systems.

- Web surfing: Addresses for porn, gambling, sports, shopping, and other sites an employee might visit when he should be working.

> Unless you can hack your way in and out of the Pentagon's computer system without being caught, you don't stand a chance of outwitting these programs. Save the extracurricular activities for home. You might save your job.

One last warning. If you have to send something sensitive in an e-mail, check and double-check the address (at work, triple-check it). Rob, an English professor in the Midwest, offers two cautionary tales: a dean at his university forwarded an e-mail about a nasty tenure battle to one of the participants by mistake, and a philosophy professor accidentally posted sensitive personnel comments to the university's bulletin board. The absentminded professors soon learned that Computer Services couldn't put the electronic genie back in the bottle.

Keeping Up Appearances

Laurel, a kind, soft-spoken doctor in Chicago, turns into a virtual Mr. Hyde when she sits down at the keyboard. She does all her writing in capital letters because, as she says, she's too busy "TO HIT THE SHIFT THINGY."

We love her dearly, but as anyone who's been online for five minutes knows, writing in all caps is considered SHOUTING. By universal acclamation, shouting has been declared a no-no. Whether you agree or not, it's a fact of life online: Shouters are seen as rude and in-your-face.

This isn't an arbitrary rule of etiquette, like not wearing white shoes after Labor Day or not eating peas with a fish fork. The real reason people find uppercase writing irritating is that it's hard to read.

Most people who write big aren't doing it to be bad. They probably find it easier to ignore the "shift thingy." It's even been speculated that some older folks use caps because they think of e-mail as a form of telegram. Whatever the reason, using all caps bugs readers and gives them eye strain.

E-mail that's all lowercase or without punctuation is almost as annoying. A capital letter now and then helps us read, by showing where sentences begin and which words are proper names. A smallish name—Ann or Bob, for instance—is almost lost in unpunctuated lowercase print (*when you review the project with ann tell bob*).

A screenful of type without paragraph breaks is no fun to read, either. It's monotonous and tiring and, again, hard on the eyes. Dividing an e-mail into indented paragraphs makes it easier to understand. Some writers even leave a blank line between paragraphs to make the divisions stand out more. Why not?

While you're at it, resist the temptation to show off typographically with bizarre lettering or graphics or spelling or punctuation. Computer jocks love this. Our techie friend Jude, a recovered typoholic, says they're the guys "who figured out how to spell 'hell' on the calculator by turning it upside down and typing '1134' and have stayed at that level of maturity."

Write like a grown-up and skip the fancy formatting. It's hard to read, and may come out as gibberish if the reader's software is incompatible. A virtual mensch makes things easy on the reader in any way he can.

Rejection Slips

Telling people no is never easy, but telling them no in an e-mail is especially tricky. People don't read e-mail as carefully as letters, and they may see a gentle rejection as encouragement or a blunt one as a slap in the face.

That's a real problem these days. A newspaper editor tells us that ninety percent of the job applications she sees arrive by e-mail. If she turns someone down too firmly, he may take offense. But if she's too sympathetic, he'll think he still has a chance; he may reduce his salary demands or send more references and samples of his work.

"I started out by being too nice," she says. "Now I'm as firm as possible without being insulting." She doesn't slam the door, though she leaves no doubt that it's been closed: "I'm sorry, but your experience does not meet our requirements." True, it stings. However, you don't do anybody a favor by leaving him with false hopes.

A friend in the corporate world finds it difficult to turn down e-mailers who ask her for time-consuming favors. We're not very good at it, either.

Many e-mailers, it seems, are as casual about their manners as they are about their writing. Someone who wouldn't dream of imposing in a letter won't hesitate in an e-mail. He'll send a busy sales manager a hyperlink to his nephew's interactive game site and ask for a marketing plan—gratis, of course. Or he'll e-mail three years of TurboTax records to his CPA cousin and ask for free advice about incorporating a wine bar.

All this comes unannounced, naturally, and the e-mailer assumes you have nothing better to do with your workday. What's more, he expects a quick reply. When he doesn't get one, he pesters you for it. He can send an e-mail instantaneously, so he thinks the reply should be instantaneous, too.

How do you say no to an inconsiderate e-mailer?

First, don't ignore his message, even if you didn't ask for it and he has no right to expect a reply. Not responding only results in irritating reminders and ill will.

Second, don't be too harsh or too gentle when you do respond. Try to find a middle ground: *I can't help you, because I know almost nothing about video games and even less about marketing them.* Or: *My specialty isn't corporate taxes, but I'd be happy to refer you to another accountant.*

The Prurient Express

Did you hear about the young solicitor who sent copies of his girlfriend's X-rated e-mail to colleagues at his sober British law firm? They e-mailed the message to others, and before you could say "Rumpole of the Bailey," the poor girl's sex life was public knowledge from London to Hong Kong. Besieged by the press, she went into hiding. Her boyfriend? He and his indiscreet friends were disciplined for sending personal e-mail at work.

Romance in the workplace was a fact of life long before e-mail. (Come to think of it, the two of us met on the job.) But the computer has made it easier to be imprudent, as well as to get caught at it. Employers will never keep romance out of the office—or out of the office computer. However, they can expect an employee to show discretion and common sense when he e-mails his main squeeze.

Even a company that frowns on personal e-mail would probably let you get away with an innocent message like this: *It was a great evening. Let's do it again on Friday.* You'd be smart, though, to leave out the juicy details: *I always wondered what you'd look like without your clothes, and now I know. Va-va-voom! (P.S.: The whipped cream was a nice touch.)*

Don't e-mail anything you wouldn't want to share with the whole office—or for that matter, the whole industry. Every week or so there's something in the news about an employee who's sacked because he can't resist e-mailing office buddies about his sexploits. One young financial genius blithely messaged friends at work about the "hot chicks" he'd scored with. The e-mail was forwarded to thousands of people on Wall Street and, you guessed it, he lost his job.

If e-mail in the office can be too intimate, e-mail outside the office isn't always intimate enough. A college student from our town thinks people often use e-mail to distance themselves and avoid intimacy. "You can more easily just blow it off," she says. Many singles these days give out e-mail addresses instead of phone numbers to keep potential dates at arm's length. It takes only an e-mail or two to size somebody up, and a no is easier to deliver by computer than over the phone.

But in the virtual world, as in the real one, some people don't take no gracefully. Sophie, a teenage friend, was in a chat room some time ago and bumped into a jerk called Michelangelo. Six months later, he was still pestering her with e-mails. "Needless to say," she told us, "I haven't been in a chat room since."

Unwanted romantic overtures can be a pain, but you don't have to swear off chat rooms, newsgroups, or other online communities. Instead of using your regular screen name, create an ID strictly for schmoozing. Keep your two lives separate, at least until you're sure the person at the other end is someone you want to know for real.

2. All's Well That Sends Well
Anatomy of an E-Mail

Talk about words coming back to haunt you! We found a Web site that lets you send e-mail that won't be opened until after you're dead. Of course, most of us would like our e-mail read sometime before that. But the fact is that plenty of e-mail is read later rather than sooner, if it's read at all.

E-mails are ridiculously easy to send, and even easier to delete—or ignore like electronic dust bunnies in a messy in-box. Anybody who wants his e-mail read while he's still vertical should learn the realities of computer life.

E-mail's greatest strength is that it combines the best of two worlds: the convenience of a phone call and the permanence of a letter. That's also its greatest weakness.

Like the phone, it's fast, it's brief, it's spontaneous, and it's informal. Like a letter, it can be polished, copied, forwarded, stored, and answered when you get around to it. But speed is dangerous. Brevity can be abrupt, spontaneity sloppy. Informality isn't always appropriate. And the convenience features can backfire, too. Imagine a tax lawyer accidentally forwarding a client's list of hidden assets to the IRS. Or a Stalinesque boss coming across an old office e-mail that referred to his wife as a "bosomy dirty-book writer."

We trip up when we forget that e-mail is a hybrid. Usually the problem is that we treat it too much like a phone call and not enough like a letter.

Those who use e-mail like a phone tend to skip the courtesies. They don't edit themselves, and to hell with grammar and spelling and punctuation. They don't form complete sentences or divide the message into paragraphs. They don't reread what they've written before hitting Send. They forget that other eyes may read it months or even years later. Okay, e-mail is spontaneous and informal, but it's still writing, and any piece of writing that's badly done—abrupt, disorganized, confusing, hard to read, difficult to follow, indiscreet—doesn't work.

No doubt it's natural that people should take e-mail for granted, since it seems to be everywhere nowadays. Even if you've never posted to a bulletin board for migraine sufferers or chatted online about the best zinnias for Zone 7, sold a Willie Mays card on eBay or contributed a *Chicken Soup* review to Amazon.com, you've probably written e-mail. If not, you've been in hibernation or on sabbatical to Pluto (or maybe you're one of the shrinking "I don't do e-mail" crowd).

E-mail has become such a part of our lives that many people don't think of it as writing. In fact, they don't think about it at all. They just do it. And therein lies the trouble. The less trouble they take with their e-mail, the more trouble they give their readers.

The things that go wrong with e-mail are the same things that go wrong with any other kind of writing. Maybe the writer doesn't know his subject, or doesn't keep the audience in mind, or doesn't use clear language. Perhaps the message is poorly written, misspelled, unpunctuated, hard to understand, or comes from . . . *do I know this person?* In the chapters ahead we'll talk more about polishing the writing itself. First let's look at the parts of an e-mail and how to make them work for you.

Identity Crisis

A college professor we know—let's call him Tibor—used to delete any e-mail with "Hotmail" in the address, on the mistaken assumption that it must be coming from a porn site. For months, he obliterated innocent messages right and left, until one of his students enlightened him. The lesson? An e-mail address (say, Boogers@Yahoo.com or Toynbee@Harvard.edu) can tell a lot about the sender, not all of it true.

Skinner on Behavior

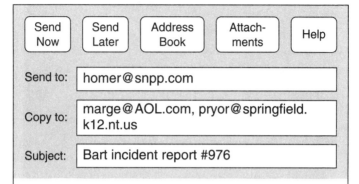

I regret having to disturb you at the Springfield Nuclear Power Plant, Mr. Simpson, but this time your son has gone too far. Today he flooded the school gym with a fire hose, then surfed the basketball court on a backboard. A harmless prank (e.g., bra-snapping or Xeroxing his butt) is one thing, but major property damage is another.

While I am of the opinion that Bart is possessed by demons, Dr. Pryor, the district psychiatrist, informs me that the boy is in fact suffering from Attention Deficit Hyperactivity Disorder. Be that as it may, Bart will be expelled unless you agree to treatment with Ritalin or another appropriate psychotropic substance. Will you and your wife stop by at 10 tomorrow morning to discuss the matter? Thank you.

Principal Seymour Skinner,
Springfield Elementary School
(skinner@springfield.k12.nt.us)

Take the user name, the part of the address before @. A goofy name (like Lipstyx or Vampira) may be fine if you're e-mailing the hunk you met at Home Depot, though you wouldn't want to use it to message a business contact. A good screen name is hard to find, and growing harder as more people go online, but it's worth the trouble to get one. The name you choose sends a signal about your personality.

The same can be said of the domain name, the info that comes after @ (as in CIA.gov or Tulane.edu). It identifies the kind of Internet account you have: educational (".edu"), commercial (".com"), governmental (".gov"), and so on. A research fellow e-mailing an academic he doesn't know might be smart to use his ".edu" address at Tulane rather than his daughter's ".com" account at AOL. True, the campus plumber, as well as an associate dean, might use ".edu" in his address. Just keep in mind that you're often judged by the small things.

You can't always control your e-mail address. At work, you'll probably be using your company's domain name, and your employer may limit your choice of a user name. But when you have a say in picking your address, consider what your address says about you.

From Deleted to Delovely

As we were working on this chapter, our friend Gloria, a librarian, sent us an e-mail with the subject line "Joke—and more." Now, Gloria is someone who speaks her mind, and there's usually no doubt about what she means. Naturally, we assumed from the subject line that her message was largely a joke, and left it unopened for two or three days while we responded to mail that seemed more important.

When we finally got around to Gloria's, we were appalled we'd waited so long. Sure, her message began with a throwaway joke, but it continued with several pages of earth-shattering (well, sort of) news. She was quitting her job after more than twenty years and packing up to take another one in a different city. She'd already found a new house, for crying out loud.

We called to apologize for not tuning in sooner.

If you want your e-mail read promptly, use a subject line that does justice to your message. We would have opened Gloria's much faster if she'd used something like "Stop the presses!" or "7.5 on the Richter scale" or "I'm outta here."

Delayed is one thing; deleted is another. The quickest way to get your message deleted before it's even read is to begin with a subject line that has the faint, or not so faint, aroma of spam. This is especially true if you're writing to someone who doesn't recognize your address.

In the good old days of the information revolution, back in the twentieth century, we used to consider all incoming e-mail innocent until proven guilty. We opened everything. Then one day we clicked on a sales pitch that gave our hard drive the flu. Now we zap anything that looks spammy ("Lose weight by eating" or "Earn a Ph.D. in your sleep" or "Borrow your way to riches"). Many people we know do the same thing. They don't want to waste time on spam or, worse, pick up a virus from a malicious e-mail.

If you're e-mailing somebody who may not know your address, be sure to make clear in the subject line that your message is for real. State your name or your business or why the e-mail should be read: *Request from Rufus T. Firefly* or *New viaduct for Fredonia* or *Found your briefcase, Captain Spalding.*

If you don't want an urgent message to sit for a week in somebody's in-box, be specific in the subject line. Instead of writing simply, "A question," ask the question: *How do I take a Rottweiler's temperature?* Instead of "Help," get to the point: *My FedEx package is ticking!* On the other hand, if your mail doesn't need attention right away, say so in the subject line: *No hurry* or *Read after work* or *This can wait till Monday.*

When you're e-mailing busy people, keep in mind that the typical electronic mailbox looks like Broadway at rush hour. If every e-mail had a more helpful subject line, we'd all have an easier time managing our in-baskets.

A final word on the subject. If two or more people share the same e-mail address, be clear about who should get the message. Suppose you're writing to the Addamses@Woodlawn.cem with a message for the lady of the house. Mention her in the subject line: *For Morticia from Rusty Stiletto.*

Body Language

Did you ever get a twelve-page e-mail from your mom, updating you on the Siamese's bowel movements, the egg that blew up in the microwave, the two-for-one special at Publix, and a few dozen other things? You didn't find time to finish it until she messaged you a week later with the arrival time of her flight.

Far be it from us to give you advice, Mom, but here goes: If you have something important to say in an e-mail, say it. Don't bury the good stuff. When we worked for newspapers, we learned that the most important news goes first and the least important goes last. If something has to be cut at the last minute, or if the reader doesn't have time to finish, nothing important is missed. This is a good way to organize your e-mails, too.

Remember that an e-mail isn't a letter. A letter can be savored at leisure, but an e-mail's air of immediacy requires that you come to the point right away. You don't have to be impolite or forget the small courtesies. Simply don't put the breaking news at the end.

We'll have more to say in the chapters to come about improving your online writing, but we'd like to make another point here. The shorter the e-mail, the sooner it's read. Long e-mails tend to be put off till later. That doesn't mean leaving out what needs to be said; it means not saying the same thing in two or three different ways. If Bertie Wooster were e-mailing Jeeves to ask him to iron his violet cummerbund, it would be enough to say: *Jeeves, be a good egg and steam out those wrinkles in the violet cummerbund.* There's no need to add: *The old sash could use a bit of the Jeevesian touch, don't you think? Unless I'm mistaken, it still bears traces of last night's revelry at the Drones' Club.*

Answering Service

How many times has someone answered one of your e-mails with a cryptic "Go for it" or "No way" or "Ask me later"? Kind of leaves you hanging, doesn't it? Maybe your original e-mail covered lots of ground, and you don't know which part of the territory the reply is coming from. Or maybe your e-mail bounced dozens of times to dozens of people, and you don't know which bounce you're on.

The reader shouldn't have to guess what you're replying to, especially when the response is delayed and the subject line is no help ("Re: A suggestion" or "Re: The meeting"). The best solution is to rewrite the subject line that pops up when you click Reply, making it more specific (*About your logo suggestion* or *More on the logo meeting*).

Another solution is to jog the reader's memory early in the message with a few words (*About your idea for the new logo...*) or with a quote from his original e-mail. Don't quote his whole message, though, if you're replying to only part of it.

Countless people have told us they're teed off by replies that include their original e-mails, along with the techno-clutter about Return-Paths, X-Mailers, Message-ID's, MIME-Versions, Encoding, and so on. Be selective. If you click Select All when you reply to an e-mail, delete everything but the business you're actually replying to. This will make the return path smoother.

Clone Rangers

A total stranger recently sent us an e-mail accepting an invitation to a party that we weren't throwing. No, it wasn't spam, and we didn't need a Ouija board or tech support to solve the mystery.

A couple of days earlier, we'd received an invitation to the aforementioned bash from an old friend. The first two screens consisted of scores and scores of e-mail addresses. Yes, buried somewhere in the crowd was the address of our mystery e-mailer. Instead of answering only his hostess, he had clicked Reply All, so everyone who got an invitation also got his RSVP.

Oops!

Two mistakes were made here. Sure, the invitee shouldn't have hit the Reply All button. But Perle Mesta shouldn't have revealed everyone's e-mail address to everyone else on the guest list.

All right, there was a certain voyeuristic pleasure in peeking at her juicy address book. (Invitees came from such intriguing places as army.mil, usdoj.gov, uscourts.gov, mit.edu, and abc.com.) Still, how many of those people would have preferred to keep their addresses to themselves? And how many would have preferred to go right to the message without scrolling through page after page of addresses?

If you're sending an e-mail to many people, don't announce the addresses to one and all unless there's a good reason to do so (maybe you're sending a message to six department heads and you want each of them to know the others are receiving it too). When you have the time, you can e-mail each person separately, copying the same message and personalizing the salutation. When you're in a rush, most e-mail programs let you hide addresses by sending blind copies. Ours, for example, allows you to do that by putting parentheses around the address list in the Send To or Copy To spaces. The only address the recipient sees is his own.

We heard of a guy (he'll remain anonymous) who learned this lesson the hard way. He casually copied an e-mail to fifty or so of his closest friends— most of them eligible young women—to let them know his new cell-phone number. To many of the women, the list of addresses at the top looked suspiciously like a little black book. Before long they were clicking Reply All and sharing their suspicions. The jig was up.

Best Foot Forward

Several friends forwarded us a story that had been forwarded to them about a David-and-Goliath battle involving Neiman Marcus, a disgruntled customer, and a chocolate-chip cookie recipe. One version had already been forwarded five separate times to a total of 167 people, and it's probably still being forwarded through cyberspace. No doubt umpteen different versions have gone to untold e-mail addresses around the globe.

The story itself was only a little over a page long (including the recipe). But when we printed it out, complete with e-mail addresses and line after line of computer gibberish (multipart/mixed;boundary-qmail/invoked-by\quoted-printable, and so on), we used up nine pages, single-spaced.

It's tempting to click Forward when you've read

an e-mail you think a friend or colleague might enjoy. But give her a break. Go easy on the Forward button. Copy the good stuff—only the good stuff—and paste it in an e-mail. If you must forward something, add a note explaining why you're forwarding it: "Have the Publicity people seen this cookie story, and what are they doing about it?"

By the way, we enjoyed the cookie item—once we managed to find it amid the clutter. We enjoyed it even more when we learned that the story, like so many others floating around the Internet, was really fiction.

Unsuitable Attachments

Downloads don't like us, and the feeling is mutual. After one too many crashes because of incompatible software, we're wary of opening attachments. And because of the threat of a virus, we *never* accept them from strangers.

If the attachment is a document, especially a short one, we'd rather have it pasted into an e-mail. If it's a photograph, we'd prefer to have it faxed or snail-mailed. As for audio and video downloads, we'll usually pass. We use our computers for work and don't want to risk them just to download an animated St. Patrick's Day greeting card, no matter how cute.

Some of the people in our address book feel the

same way and almost never open attachments. Others love getting them—from people they know. (But then, even someone you know can unwittingly pass on a virus.)

If you want to send an attachment, check first to make sure it's welcome. Don't be offended if you're asked to send it some other way. And when you do attach something to an e-mail, say what it is: "Look at this" or "See what I found" isn't good enough, particularly when all you're sending is a photo of your hamster.

Virtually Yours

Gloria, our librarian friend, reports that her youngest daughter e-mails her constantly to look up items for school assignments. The messages usually begin without an opening and end without a closing. She once got an e-mail that started "Dear Mommy" and finished "Love, Elinor." She was so touched that she printed it out and saved it.

Like most of our grown-up friends, Gloria uses a salutation and a signature whenever she e-mails us, though she may begin with an informal "Hey" or "Hiya" and end with her initial. She's much stuffier at work, signing off with her full name, title, address, and phone number.

We're with her on this one. We nearly always start an e-mail by saying hello ("Hi, Will") and end it by saying goodbye ("See ya, Ariel"), even if we're writing to people who know our e-mail address as well as their own.

If you find salutations and signatures stiff, keep them casual. E-mails don't have to be as formal as letters. But don't get carried away at work, and that goes double if you don't know the person you're e-mailing. Maybe he'd prefer "Hi, Joe" to "Dear Mr. Stalin," but you have no way of knowing.

What if you don't know whether someone's a he or a she? Or whether she'd prefer "Miss," "Mrs.," or "Ms."? You can always fall back on the "Dear Marilyn Manson" routine. Remember to plug in the right names if you're flying on auto format. Michelle, a friend who works in publishing, tells us she often gets e-mail addressed to "Dear First Name Last Name."

When you say goodbye at the end of an e-mail by using an abbreviation like TIA (for "Thanks in advance") or TAFN ("That's all for now"), be sure your reader knows what it means. If you and your boss are happy saying MYSE ("May you see Elvis") at the end of e-mails to each other, by all means do it. When in doubt, spell it out. Instead of "TT" or "g/g," write "Ta-ta" or "Got to go." What are a few extra keystrokes? (There's more about abbreviations in chapter 4.)

If the reader doesn't know you, a signature is more than just a nice touch. David, an author, likes to hear from his fans but is ticked off when an e-mail comes in without the name of the sender, especially a message requiring a reply. "How am I supposed to address my salutation in response?" he wonders. "Am I old-fashioned for thinking that it is discourteous to ask a favor of someone without revealing your name?"

When you use a signature, it shouldn't be so precious that you're the only one who understands it. A cousin of Pat's (his initials are BB) used to sign his e-mails with two periods. To be honest, we never noticed until he told us he'd changed his signature. The two periods were supposed to represent the ammo (..) for a BB gun. Who knew?

Bumper Stickers

Some people love to add tag lines—interesting quotes, facts, jokes, and so on—to their signatures. Others aren't so fond of them.

David, the author we just mentioned, updates the brief, amusing tag lines on his e-mail every week with a favorite food, movie, book, whatever. The afterthoughts make his e-mail personal and current.

Then there's Liz, a college professor who finds long, windy tag lines, like long answering-machine recordings, a pain in the butt. She often prints out messages, and hates wasting time, paper, and ink on an interminable quotation from Kierkegaard or a drawing of the Leaning Tower of Pisa, cleverly rendered in ampersands.

As we see it, there's nothing wrong with a witty tag line at the end of an e-mail, especially if, like David, you change it every once in a while. But don't go on and on, and certainly not if you're e-mailing a tagophobe like Liz.

3. To E or Not to E
When Online's Out of Line

Harvey, a management consultant, tells about the day he stepped into a client's office to have a word with him. The man suddenly remembered an e-mail Harvey had sent him on another subject. He then turned to his keyboard and e-mailed a reply, even though Harvey was sitting only three feet away.

No wonder so many electronic mailboxes are bursting at the seams, and people are logging on from home to stay on top of mail they didn't get to at the office. E-mail is terrific, all right, but let's not make a religion of it.

A poll not long ago showed that more and more people are taking laptops with them on vacation to keep up with their office e-mail. It's not that they're workaholics. They just can't relax knowing that awaiting them back at work is the in-box from hell.

Show a little mercy for your stressed-out colleagues and consider other ways to communicate. In business as well as personal life, there are times when a phone call, a fax, a letter, a paper memo, or a face-to-face meeting would be more efficient and appropriate. A very short phone call can often do the job of a very long e-mail or several small ones. And think about leaving that laptop behind the next time you want to get away from it all.

Nerd Mentality

An old friend uses e-mail to communicate with the other lawyers in his firm, except for one holdout, a partner who won't turn on his computer and insists on having paper instead. Is he on a power trip? Is he a throwback to the days when real men didn't type and only secretaries (that is, women) worked the keyboards? Or is he insecure about his computer skills?

Whatever the motive, some people simply don't like e-mail, even in the most wired of offices. You'll only irritate them by communicating in cyberspace when you could just as well have called or written a note or walked over for a chat. They may eventually come around, but for now they'll use e-mail grudgingly. In the meantime, humor them—definitely if they're higher up the ladder than you are.

At the other extreme are the e-mail addicts who think there's no other way to communicate. They remind us of a joke making the rounds in the ether: You know you're addicted to the Internet when you wake up at three a.m. to go to the bathroom and stop to check your e-mail on the way back to bed. Let's be honest. Haven't we all done it?

In truth, some people *do* seem addicted to their computers and can't seem to connect without them, even when e-mail isn't called for. But certain kinds of office communications should not be consigned to cyberspace. A letter, a phone call, or a face-to-face conversation would be better for things like these:

- An employee evaluation, especially if it's negative.
- A request for a raise or a promotion.
- A resignation notice.
- A report of employee wrongdoing.
- Praise for a job well done.
- Criticism for a job done badly.
- Office rumors or gossip.

What's wrong with e-mailing in those cases? Well, criticism of someone can go astray and embarrass both of you if it lands in the wrong mailbox. Tooting your own horn—say, in a request for a raise—can make you look like a conceited twit if your message goes public. Juicy gossip can be traced back to the source, so save it for lunch. And using e-mail to ask a favor or pat a colleague on the back can seem inadequate.

When someone's done a great job, it's too easy to send a virtual compliment. Why not a real one? A brief conversation, in person or over the phone, or a handwritten note is much warmer and makes more of an impression.

An Oeuf Is an Oeuf

A literary agent of our acquaintance is a gentleman of the old school: thoughtful, soft-spoken, discreet, courteous. And he has online manners to match. But somehow, he laments, his attempts at dot-comedy don't always come off. There was the time an author asked him why another book on the same subject was a bestseller and his wasn't. He flippy e-mailed back: "Because it sold more copies." He lost the client.

Online humor is no joke. The scientists and engineers who made the PC a household appliance couldn't have imagined the laff-riot they were creating. Thanks to the Internet, there are more funny stories told on any given Wednesday than in the entire history of the pre-wired world. Or just about.

It was probably inevitable that cyberspace would start to resemble one long laugh track. Shy people often find that the arm's-length atmosphere of the virtual world unleashes their inner Seinfeld. Compulsive types enjoy copying long lists of jokes and forwarding them to everyone in their address books. (Hey, if one joke is funny, why not thirty-five? And if one person might like it, why not one hundred fifty?) Forwarding a joke to a friend you haven't e-mailed in

months is a handy and noncommittal means of staying in touch—get in, make contact, get out.

But there are negatives, too. A sensitive reader
may think that a forwarded joke doesn't count as real
communication, and maybe he's right. It takes no effort to hit Forward and pass on a cute story with no
personal comments from you. The gesture looks even
more offhand if you haven't bothered to delete the
cyberjunk that came with the original.

And those strings of jokes start looking awfully
familiar, don't they? Some of them float around the
Net like so much orbiting space debris, periodically
reappearing in your mailbox when somebody new
discovers them.

Obviously, online humor can have serious conse-
quences. The wrong crack, sent at the wrong time
and to the wrong person, can be a disaster. Telling a
joke face to face is one thing; e-mailing it is quite another. You don't see the person you're e-mailing, so
you can't read her body language and sense how she's
reacting. That's why some people who are wonderful
raconteurs in person have two left feet—or is it left
brains?—when they tell a funny story online.

If you have a chance, ask someone else to read
your online humor before you send it, especially when
you're trying to be ironic or tongue-in-cheek. And
don't count on Mr. Smiley Face to bail you out. When
a joke doesn't work—when it falls flat or (shudder)
offends—adding a funny emoticon or a lots-of-

laughs abbreviation only makes it worse. If you have to elbow your reader in the ribs to show her how funny the joke is, maybe it isn't.

We like a good laugh as much as the next guy and have enjoyed our share of online humor over the years. Pat has a fondness for jokes that begin with animals walking into bars. Not everyone shares that particular enthusiasm, though, so she's selective about what she passes on. (She recently sent a few connoisseurs a gem about an octopus that tries to hit on a set of bagpipes in a saloon.)

How do you discourage unwanted humor? If you've found a gracious way, let us know. We just grin and bear it. A friend in Arizona is on a former secretary's mailing list and regularly gets jokes from her of the "Take my wife . . . please" variety. As a liberated guy, he's unamused. He'd like to be off her list, but doesn't want to hurt her feelings. His solution: Delete the gags without reading them.

Humor is a very individual thing, and nothing sent to everyone on your mailing list will be equally delightful to all. When in doubt, don't.

Courtesy Calls

We consider ours an equal-opportunity household, where the chores are unisex and the division of labor is fifty-fifty. But Pat has always done the social correspondence—the birthday and anniversary cards, holiday greetings, bread-and-butter notes, and such.

So has the computer revolution transformed the way Pat handles the social niceties? Has she put down the fountain pen and the stamps and the personal stationery and gone digital?

Not yet—or not entirely. Like most people, she's somewhere in the middle on using e-mail for the bread-and-butter stuff. However, minds are rapidly changing. Friends who would never have sent us a thank-you note by e-mail a year ago now feel it's all right . . . sometimes.

Admittedly, an e-mail courtesy note is a fast and cheap and easy way to send thanks or congratulations or sympathy. Still more tempting and convenient are online greeting cards. Web sites offer a staggering array of colorful, musical, sometimes animated cards for everything from the usual festive occasions to downers like divorce, job loss, bankruptcy, even death.

What's fast and cheap and easy isn't always fitting, though. An electronic thank you may seem proper in one case but not in another: "Thanks for lunch," but not "Thanks for the bone marrow transplant." Many people don't appreciate online cards as much as real ones. What to do? Here are a few considerations.

First, the more important and solemn the occasion, the less appropriate a virtual message will be. When someone dies, an adequate expression of sympathy isn't just a click away. It's fine to send an e-mail letting family members know you've heard the bad news and your thoughts are with them. Still, follow up with a handwritten message and a real card, not a virtual one.

Second, the more formal the relationship, the less appropiate the e-greeting. An online birthday card might tickle the socks off your roommate or carpool buddy, but if you're thanking the boss for a wedding gift, virtual isn't close enough. When you don't know someone well, an online greeting can seem impersonal, a way of putting distance between you.

Third, think of conditions at the receiving end. The mail system where your boyfriend works may choke on a twelve-course attachment. Besides, he might not want everyone within earshot to hear that snappy rendition of "Light My Fire."

Finally, some people would much rather listen to your voice or read your words on paper. They don't think to check their e-mail, so sending them messages doesn't get you anywhere. Stewart's analog brother, Larry, has a virtual address he never uses. The only way to e-mail a greeting to him is through his teen-age son.

Keep in mind that a letter sometimes carries more weight than an e-mail, as many parents are finding out. Mike, a newspaper editor, regularly e-mails his kids at college, but he prefers an old-fashioned letter when he's in what he calls his "Dispensing Good Advice mode." It gets their attention, and it's cheaper than a singing telegram.

Face Time

When the medium is e-mail, the message can be bad for the bottom line, as many companies are learning. E-mail misunderstandings aren't merely awkward; they waste time, cost money, and interfere with work. Trying to settle them by e-mail may aggravate matters. A meeting or a phone call is often faster and more effective.

You've probably witnessed a scene like this. The boss walks by somebody's desk and says in passing, "Take a look at the article on nouvelle marketing in this morning's paper." From the tone of her voice, it's obvious she's only dropping a casual remark.

Now imagine a different scene. The same remark, delivered in a toneless e-mail, looks ominous and threatening. "Oh God, she wants us to overhaul the department!" the employee thinks. In a panic, he overreacts and spends the rest of the afternoon drawing up a new organization plan.

Asking an e-mail to carry your message is sometimes asking a lot. Words all by themselves, staring out from a computer screen, may not be enough. In a face-to-face meeting, body language, tone of voice, and facial expressions help people communicate. In a phone call, voice cues and back-and-forth exchanges can prevent misunderstandings. And a "real" letter, with its traditional courtesies, may make a better impression.

In fact, some major corporations are asking their e-mail-addicted employees to work more face time into their day. How? By going over to someone and moving their lips. Give it a try. It's good for business.

Multiple Listings

A senior-management type told us the other day about a corporate veep who was so overwhelmed by e-mail that he had his computer automatically delete any messages copied or forwarded to him.

That might seem extreme, but consider this. The guy had several thousand people working for him, and a good number of them felt the need to keep him informed of their every move. Naturally, he couldn't keep up. Who could?

The moral of the story? Don't clog up the supervisor's mailbox by copying or forwarding things he doesn't have to see. Yes, you'd like him to know how hard you're working, but he won't appreciate all those copies if he has to spend evenings and weekends reading them at home.

E-mail can be a great efficiency tool. But e-mail overload can eat up the workday and reduce productivity. Increasingly, managers are asking employees to e-mail them only when necessary and to do it directly—no copies or forwards, please. The more time they spend looking at unnecessary e-mail, the less work they get done.

You don't have to be a boss to drown in copied or forwarded e-mail. Many co-workers are too quick to share their messages with one another. If you have something that should be shared, e-mail it directly or, perhaps, try the phone.

Another thing that ticks people off is all the extra garbage—routing messages, strings of addresses, and such—that comes with copies and forwards. So hold the mayo, and paste only the relevant material into a fresh e-mail.

At home, the techno-litter can be irritating too. Give friends and relatives a break. Clean up your act and send them only what's welcome.

Whether you're e-mailing someone who's at home or at work, don't send a sumo-sized attachment unless you know she wants it and her computer can handle it. (You'll find more about copying, forwarding, and downloads in chapter 2.)

Note: Nobody we know likes chain letters, especially those that begin, "This is not a chain letter." Any e-mail that asks you to copy it and send it along to other people is a chain letter. At best, it's an imposition. Usually it's pushy and obnoxious. At worst, when you're asked to send money in hopes of getting more back, it's illegal.

Pass the Spam

Rachel, a music producer in Manhattan, goes ballistic whenever a delivery guy sticks a handful of take-out menus under her door to drum up business. To her, it's an invasion of privacy. We weren't bothered too much by menu proliferation when we lived in the city. Some menus came in handy, and we tossed out the rest.

We don't have conniptions over junk e-mail, either. The two of us regularly delete spam without reading it whenever we go online. To keep the junk to a minimum, we use an industrial-strength mail filter on our main screen name, and switch to other ID's when we send messages to bulletin boards and the like.

Most people we know, however, feel about spam the way Rachel feels about those unwanted menus. It sends them into orbit. So remember the anti-spam majority anytime the entrepreneurial spirit strikes you, particularly when you're thinking of sending promotional messages to strangers or to online communities.

If you absolutely must plug that ergonomic mouse or rutabaga cookbook, the litter of wirehaired dachshunds or the exercise bike that measures vital signs, be considerate. Imagine yourself staring at the monitors of the folks who'll open the message.

What annoys people most about junk mail is that it's indiscriminate. The spammer bombards the virtual world with thousands of identical, unsolicited messages with the aim of hitting a few targets by chance. Unfortunately, thousands of innocent bystanders are hit, too. Besides clogging up electronic mailboxes and driving people nuts, those "Get rich quick" and "Lose weight fast" messages slow down the info highway and increase costs for everyone who logs on.

The line between spam and legitimate promotion isn't always clear. Blindly sending bulk mail is definitely a no-no, but does every message have to be one-on-one? Now for some ideas about how to promote your pet project without being obnoxious.

- Instead of e-mailing a sales pitch to perfect strangers, send it to friends or clients who might be interested in your cookbook. Ask them to get the word out to other rutabaga lovers. Be sure to thank them profusely and apologize for the trouble you're putting them to. You're asking a big favor.
- Send messages to discussion groups only if their members might reasonably be interested in what you're plugging. A mailing list that deals with repetitive strain injuries, for example, might be a good place to make the case for that ergonomic mouse.
- Avoid sending identical messages to more than one online community. Not every word has to change, but the subject line and some of the text should be customized for each audience.
- Keep hype out of the subject line. "Litter of Wire-haired Dachshunds" is plenty. Saying "Reserve Your Champion-to-Be" is too spammy and doesn't tell readers anything about the pups.

- Get personal. Instead of posting a message about your exercise bike to misc.fitness.aerobic, search for a posting about exercise equipment, perhaps one asking for the name of a bike that monitors vital signs, and reply to that message.

Lighten up while you're at it. The harder the sell, the harder the sale.

Flame Fatale

We were looking at a newsgroup for pet owners when we spotted a message from someone who had bought health insurance for his geriatric dog. Someone else jumped in and expressed outrage that a pet could get health insurance when a lot of hardworking people couldn't.

Uh-oh, we thought. Here comes a flame war. That's what happens when members of an online community fire heated messages at one another until the temperature in la-la land reaches 110 in the shade.

In this case, war was averted. The critic turned down the heat by adding that his remarks weren't intended as a flame. The dog owner then agreed that it was unfair for working people to go uninsured, but he went on to explain his point of view. He was a retired World War II veteran who'd worked for sixty years and felt he had the right to take good care of his dog if he could afford to.

"Spend it, my friend, you deserve it," the former critic responded. "Good luck in your retirement."

An online community is a terrific place to find like-minded people and share experiences. But it's also a hothouse for grouches, where people can vent without fear of having their faces rearranged. Tempers escalate at microprocessor speeds. Molehills become mountains. Voilà—a flame war is born.

It doesn't have to happen. Here's how to handle flammable material.

Don't post in anger to online communities. Sleep on it. If you feel the same way the next day, send a reasoned message instead of a flame. Don't get testy, and don't get personal.

When you've been flamed, resist the temptation to answer in kind. If the person is a jerk, you won't achieve anything by descending to his level. Besides, maybe he didn't intend any offense, so why start a flame war because he misunderstood you or expressed himself clumsily? A gentle explanation may be in order. You'll never make him see your point unless you address him calmly.

If you do criticize someone or respond to criticism, consider doing it in an e-mail instead. Why involve the whole discussion group?

In writing to an online community, you're addressing everybody in the group, not just the jerk. He may deserve a verbal kick in the keister, but that doesn't mean you have to deliver it in public. Don't say anything in a virtual community that you wouldn't say in a real one. (If you're the jerk, check out one of the anger-management sites on the Web.)

Incidentally, if you must be critical online, get your facts straight. Many "experts" don't. Most of the grammar flames we've seen, for instance, have grammar mistakes themselves, and many even misspell the word "grammar." Ain't it a shame?

Buddy Count

Instant messages are the fast food of online communication. You can't beat them for instant gratification. But not everyone likes Chicken McNuggets. And not many people—not of voting age, anyway—would want them as a steady diet.

Our teenage nephew Craig (a Wendy's fan) introduced us to instant messages some years back. In fact, he introduced us to quite a few of them. Every time we logged on, it seemed, there he was. Before long, more and more people had caught the bug. We were moonbeamed nonstop. It was impossible to get any work done online. Eventually, we decided to block all instant messages.

We're learning to live with the guilt. So are many others. What began as a kid thing has spread like kudzu, invading home and office computers from the redwood forests to the Gulf Stream waters. What's fun at home, though, can be a royal pain at work.

An instant message isn't an itty-bitty e-mail. It's more like a phone call. An e-mail can be read and answered at your convenience, but an IM announces itself with a jingle, like a ringing telephone. It's in your face, insisting on attention *now.*

People who wouldn't dream of phoning someone at the office on her busiest day of the week will IM her without a second thought. That tinkly instant message, however, is just as much of an interruption as a ringing phone. Maybe more so. If she can't take a call, her voice mail can, and nobody's feelings are hurt. If she ignores an instant message, the sender knows she's there and may feel snubbed. She can't win.

We're not saying that instant messages ought to be banned from the workplace. When speed is of the essence (in closing an important deal or signing off on an urgent report), not much beats instant messages. Companies are also finding them handy for virtual business conferences, which save a mint on transportation and hotel expenses. Even some of the judges in the Microsoft antitrust case used laptops to IM their law clerks from the bench.

But be judicious. Consider an e-mail instead of an instant message when you connect with someone at the office (remember, a home office is an office, too). And if you do IM, begin by asking whether the person is free to respond. Don't be insulted if the answer is no.

4. Accustomed to Your Interface
Keeping the Reader in Mind

We still get a laugh out of that old *New Yorker* cartoon of two dogs at a desktop computer. "On the Internet," one explains to the other, "nobody knows you're a dog."

Computer users aren't really anonymous online, but they often write as if they were. Something about the virtual world makes them forget they're writing to real people.

Whether you're sending an e-mail or an instant message, posting to a bulletin board or updating a Web page, somebody out there will be reading. Your boss? Your teenage son? The Neanderthal whose pickup truck you scratched in the parking lot? Just as you don't speak the same way to your boss as you do to your teenager (if you're on speaking terms with the kid at all), you should adjust your online writing style to your audience.

Yeah, yeah, you say, everyone knows that. Well, everyone may know it, but not everyone does it.

Losing sight of the audience leads to klutzy communication. What's true in the dressing room is true online: One size does not fit all.

Call Me Modem

Before putting your first words on the screen, take a minute to size up your reader. Does he know about the stock split, or is he out of the loop? Is she an animal-rights militant, or does she like to flaunt her fur? Is he still sensitive about his divorce? Is she the life of the party or a stick-in-the-mud? Does he leave his sentences half finished? Does she go ballistic over grammar and spelling goofs? Spelling may not be all that important on a family Web page (unless Dad is an English teacher or Sis won the National Spelling Bee), but it should be up to snuff on your company's tech-support site.

Make a mental picture of the reader—her likes and dislikes, age and education, his strengths and weaknesses, personality and peeves—then customize your vocabulary and style with him or her in mind. You wouldn't use the same hip-hop slang in an e-mail to a grumpy math professor that you'd use in an instant message to your eleven-year-old niece.

That doesn't mean you should write down to the tween, or up to the egghead. Treat them both with respect, if you want them to respect you. People have inborn BS detectors and can spot a phony before the end of the first sentence.

What if you're strangers, though? How do you make a mental picture of someone you don't know?

Chances are, you know *something*. Let's say you own a pet store and you're e-mailing a man who makes organic dog biscuits. You may not know him, but you know how much your customers like his biscuits. Build on the things you know, and never take for granted the things you don't. If you don't know his views on home schooling or the death penalty, don't spout your own unless you have a good reason.

And what if you're writing to several people, perhaps in an e-mail to the whole Accounting Department, or on a Web page for a virtual store? Try to picture one person—the guy in the corner office, or a cousin who likes to shop online. Give it a try. You'll sound more natural.

Mr. Have a Nice Day

A couple we know—they don't like publicity, so we won't use their real names—are the yin and yang of Internet writing. Nora loves the freewheeling grammar, spelling, and punctuation (or lack thereof). Nick grits his teeth and thinks online writing should be held to the same standards as the offline variety. One point they agree on is emoticons, those typographical thingies used to convey tongue-in-cheekness and other subtleties that might be lost online. Not surprisingly, they agree for entirely different reasons. Nora thinks smileys and frownies add spice to online writing, while Nick sees them as a necessary evil to help crummy writers avoid being misunderstood.

We prefer to use words, not cutesy faces, to show that we're happy or sad or kidding or ticked off. Emoticons seem too precious to us, like those tiny circles Pat used to draw over her *i*'s in the sixth grade. What's syrupy to us, however, may be sweet to you and the person you're e-mailing.

Our friend Jude, who writes about computers, doesn't use emoticons herself but says it's obvious why they're popular, especially with newbies: "They're sometimes the only friendly face you'll see as you tangle with the strange, scary new world of the PC. It's a touch of humanity, a transference of the human form into pixels."

If you find the little guys sweet or comforting or useful, then make all the smileys you want. Just remember that they have their limits. As far as we know, there's no emoticon for "to be read in a fake Viennese accent while in full field marshal regalia." And be sure the folks at the other end know what those squiggles mean. By now, anyone who's stuck a toe in the surf can tell Mr. Have a Nice Day :-) from Mr. Down in the Dumps :-(but the more digitally challenged may not know the difference between bored :-o and bummed out :-c.

Some people who frown on smileys have come up with an alternative—they insert asides between pointy brackets, as in <grins> or <hugs> or <whew>.

When Jude lashes out in an e-mail she might add
<pissy little bitch mode> to take away the sting. If she
wants to brag about something without seeming like
a braggart, she might add <bustin' my buttons>.

For now, we'll save our <hugs> for the real world.

Modem Art

Here are some of the smileys you're most likely
to see online. They come in two forms, with or
without a nose, and you have to tilt your head to
the left to read them. If these aren't enough for you,
put "emoticon" in your search engine and stand
back.

:) or :-)	Smile
:(or :-(	Frown
;) or ;-)	Wink
:D or :-D	Grin
:'(or :'-(	Sob
>:{ or >:-{	Devil
0:) or 0:-)	Angel
{ }	Hug
:*) or :-*)	Kiss
:P or :-P	Sticking out tongue

In Our Humble Opinion

In pre-digital times, when Stewart was a foreign
correspondent for United Press International, he used
telegramese to wire the home office. A phrase such as
"soon as possible," for example, would become SAP.

The news service was paying by the word, so it made sense to use an acronym—a word formed from the first letters of the words in a phrase—to save on cable fees.

Nowadays, when you can e-mail a book for the cost of a local phone call, there's no reason to telegraph your language. Yet many people are in such a hurry that they pepper their online writing with acronyms and abbreviations to save a second here, two seconds there. By the end of the day, they might actually save a whole minute.

Time is money, or so it's said, but what about the reader's time? If he's familiar with your shorthand, okay. If not, he'll spend more time trying to figure out what you mean than you'll save with the geekspeak. So before you use it, make sure your reader can translate.

Geekiness aside, some common abbreviations are shortened forms of clichés. IMHO, to cite one, is short for "in my humble opinion." Unless you really want to parade your modesty, skip the cliché and say it straight ("I think that..."). If you need convincing, imagine what a wired Joyce Kilmer might have written:

> *IMHO, I shall never see*
> *A poem lovely as a tree....*

Technically, most Internet abbreviations aren't real acronyms (an acronym, like RAM, is pronounced as a word), but wired folks tend to use the two terms interchangeably. Whatever you call it, don't assume you can say something nasty and get away with it by adding a funny abbreviation (or smiley or bracketed aside): *May your brain be infested with maggots and your entrails eaten by jackals. LOL.*

Clickety Split

Below are some of the abbreviations you'll see most often when you're online. If this list is too abbreviated for you, search the Web for "Internet acronyms" or "Internet abbreviations."

LOL	Laughing out loud
ROFL	Rolling on floor laughing
IMHO	In my humble opinion
BTW	By the way
CU	See you
FTF	Face to face
TTFN	Ta-ta for now
BRB	Be right back
BFN	Bye for now
GMTA	Great minds think alike

Kitsch and Tell

Stewart's dad, who's pushing ninety, treats the answering machine as a high-tech innovation. When he leaves us a message, he speaks s-l-o-w-l-y and c-a-r-e-f-u-l-l-y. "This is Dad, Stewart's father," he begins, in case we can't recognize the voice. At the end of his message, he signs off, "That's all for now. Love, Dad."

For him, there's a big difference between talking on the phone—which he does with great gusto—and leaving a message on the machine. He tightens up when he speaks to the machine, as if he were dictating a letter. He senses that his recorded words will live on, if only for a short time, so he chooses them more carefully.

Even people who take answering machines for granted tend to speak more formally on voice mail than in phone conversations. In real time, they don't worry so much about forgetting a name or skipping a key fact or confusing "lie" and "lay." But they're more careful—and more accurate—when they say something that will be around for a while and might be replayed several times.

A posting to a newsgroup, bulletin board, mailing list, or the like is similar in some respects to a message left on an answering machine. It's almost as casual and spontaneous as if it were spoken. Yet it, too, will be around for a while. What's more, the posting is public rather than private—the community at large can read it. For all these reasons, the message *should* be more carefully composed than something shouted from a soapbox or casually dropped into a phone conversation.

Contributions to message boards, like other kinds of online writing, become sloppy and ineffective when they're not treated like *writing*. It might help to think of something sent to an online community as a letter to the editor. Just as you can go to your local paper's Web site and find an article that appeared months ago, so you can find an old posting in a newsgroup archive. In fact, these messages are often called articles.

Think of Stewart's father. Write s-l-o-w-l-y and c-a-r-e-f-u-l-l-y. You can skip the "Love, Dad."

Gorilla Theater

Did you catch Koko the talking gorilla when she was holding forth in an AOL chat room about food, love, babies, and other primate issues? What struck us was that Koko made more sense than some of the humans we've met in chat rooms. Maybe that's because the pace was slower than usual. As Koko expostulated, a trainer translated her sign language and an assistant typed the words on a keyboard.

In a typical public chat room, with a dozen or more people tapping away at the same time, the words fly fast and loose. Some folks like the chaos, even thrive on it. We know teenagers who have no problem hanging out in several chat rooms at once, juggling umpteen conversations, keeping everybody straight, all the while eating chocolate-chip cookie dough, watching TV, and talking on the phone. The sensory overload is harder on us old-media types.

After a few minutes of trying to figure out who's saying what to whom, the aging gray cells cry uncle.

As you can tell, we're not big on chat rooms. Chataholics may be using keyboards to communicate, but whatever's going on is more like pre-writing than the real thing. Think about the opening of the movie *2001,* where the chimps are banging those bones around and haven't quite gotten the idea of using them as tools.

Much of the conversation in your typical chat room goes something like this:

Andy: *Hello, Barney.*
Barney: *Ten-four, Andy.*
Andy: *Barney, how are you?*
Barney: *Andy, how are you? Roger.*
Otis: *Hi, everybody.*
Andy: *Hello, Otis.*
Floyd: *Who's Roger? <grins>*
Gomer: *Hey, Andy. <grins>*
Aunt Bee: *Hi, everyone. <hugs>*
Gomer: *Hey, Otis. Where you been?*
Otis: *Indisposed. :-)*
Floyd: *Ha ha. LOL.*
Aunt Bee: *Where's Opie? It's almost dinnertime.*
Otis: *Anybody seen Goober?*
Opie: *Yo, Aunt Bee. What's for dinner?*
Floyd: *Goober's with Thelma Lou.*
Aunt Bee: *Liver and onions.*

Barney: *Very funny, Floyd. ROFL.*

Opie: *Can I eat at Ellie's?*

Emmett: *How's it hangin', Otis? (Scuse me, Aunt Bee.)*

Thelma Lou: *Hello all.* :-) *Is Barney there?*

Gomer: *Hey. <grins>*

Floyd: *Hey, Thelma Lou.*

Barney: *Affirmative, Thelma Lou. Roger.*

And so on.

If you want to skim the surface with some compatible types and exchange a few <hugs> and <grins> or <boos> and <hisses>, then public chat rooms are for you. But if what you want is a serious forum for the exchange of ideas, look elsewhere.

To be fair, the people in these chats aren't entirely to blame for the measly offerings. In a busy room, it's hard to get out a meaningful thought without being hopelessly left behind. Delays in typing and transmission can cause lags of several seconds or more. So you're forced to send out your ideas in short bursts (one study found that the average message was only about six words long). That means you're constantly interrupted, and if you need a couple of paragraphs to make your case, forget about it. By the time you come to the end of your spiel, the beginning is history.

Private chats, though, are another matter. Anybody with the right software can set one up. Most of these chats are undoubtedly social, but businesses and universities are finding them useful substitutes for face-to-face or phone-to-phone contacts.

A private chat is by invitation only, which means you have to know someone to get in. Since you're less likely to interrupt someone you know or step on his virtual toes, the chat is less of a free-for-all.

As for quality, crummy writing might squeak by in a private chat with a friend, but it won't do when you're chatting with an online customer or a wired economics professor. You'd have to be a CIA cryptologist (or at least a ten-year-old) to break the code when a few multitasking preteens are exchanging pleasantries in cyberspace. A professor shouldn't need a code book, however, when she holds virtual office hours with students. And a puzzled shopper shouldn't feel even more puzzled after he chats with a customer-support type.

The Webutantes' Ball

When Pat wrote a column for a Web publication, an e-zine for cyber-savvy working women, she agonized over every word. The editor had once worked with her at *The New York Times,* and the two of them labored on the piece as carefully as if it had been written for the paper of record.

When she wrote for two other Web sites, Pat didn't sweat the details. One site belonged to Sandy, a yellow Lab owned by our friends Isabel and Jeannine, and it was full of greetings from other dogs and their owners. The second Web page was devoted to our newborn niece, Haylee, and came directly from the hospital. Pat's testimonials to Sandy and Haylee didn't take hours to compose. She only made sure they were clear, ran spell-checks, and read them over for gaffes that might hurt her rep as a grammar maven.

Whether you're creating your own Web page or contributing something to someone else's, keep your audience in mind. A lousy page is usually lousy because somebody forgot who'd be reading. A Web site to keep relatives abreast of the breaking news in your life may be almost as chatty and informal as a family reunion. But an e-zine article, aimed at thousands or millions of readers, can be archived and available for years to come. The tone might be breezy and informal, but the piece should be as scrupulously written as a print article.

There's a temptation to exaggerate in e-zine writing, to get there first, to showcase rumor and innuendo, to value irreverence over fairness and style over substance. But responsible e-zine writing should be just as meticulous about the facts, just as fair, just as honest as any other journalism. Don't be merely the first to get it. Be the first to get it right.

Respect the reader, too, when creating a Web site, for home or work or school or whatever. Real people have to navigate it. Make signs and directions as legible as you can, even if that means some of the hip design has to go. A splashy site is no good if the reader can't find her way around or ends up clicking to Nowheresville.

Home pages should be clear and uncluttered, with easy-to-read type and not too much of it. If the background wallpaper shimmers and the sixties pop-psychedelic typeface pulsates and throbs, the reader may vacate the premises. And go easy on the animation and sound effects. They're not so impressive to the guy whose computer doesn't have the gigachops to handle them.

Lurk Before You Leap

Cyberville is made up of countless neighborhoods. Each nook and cranny—newsgroup, bulletin board, chat room, you name it—has its own personality, its own way of saying things.

Dangling modifiers might be corrected in one online community, while grammar flames are taboo in another. Some groups are paragons of political correctness, while others delight in incorrectness. Bathroom humor may be off-limits in one crowd but the lingua franca of another. Nothing bugs an online group more than a newbie who barges in without taking the trouble to learn about the members' likes and dislikes. In many groups, for instance, you'll be virtually tarred and feathered if you stray from the subject that brought everybody together in the first place.

You can educate yourself by checking out the

FAQ, the community's list of frequently asked questions. This can save you from bringing up something that's been dealt with a hundred times before. But often the rules are unwritten and you have to figure them out by lurking, or eavesdropping, for a while before jumping in.

Made to Order

We stumbled across a curious Web site one evening. You type something in standard English and the program translates it into dialects, like "redneck," "cockney," or "hacker." Type in, say, "Happy families are all alike; every unhappy family is unhappy in its own way." The Dialectizer can spit out a backwoods version ("Happy families is all alike; ev'ry unhappy fambly is unhappy in its own way"), or one in Netspeak ("happyy famiuleis Are a7l aliek; evary unhhappy gamilysi unahppy in itS own wsay").

Now, we're not recommending using funny—or not so funny—dialects. You're more likely to offend than to connect. But customizing your online writing is a good idea, and there are less extreme ways to go about it. Some people change the physical appearance of their messages for specific audiences. They might use a funky background for e-mailing an old friend from hippie days, or an extra-large typeface for posting to a retired watchmakers' bulletin board. In a chat room, various colors and typefaces can make it easier to tell one chatterer from another.

When you're writing to friends and family, an individual touch can be the cyber equivalent of hand-writing on deckled vellum. Nearly every e-mail program lets you use an assortment of colors and typefaces. (As far as we know, there's no virtual substitute, at least yet, for scented paper or pressed flowers.)

In business, it's a good idea to use whatever style is common in that field. If you're a tailor e-mailing a Supreme Court justice about a new line of robes, keep it straight. If you're a costume maker selling a tutu made of bananas to a performance artist, go for it. If in doubt, stick with the default styles that come with your word-processing and e-mail programs.

Whether you're writing for business or pleasure, make sure the other person's software can read any custom touches you throw in. Otherwise, those colorful flourishes may be lost in translation.

Truth or Consequences

Feathers were ruffled in a newsgroup for bird-watchers when the binocular gang noticed that CBS was using canned birdcalls to liven its coverage of golf tournaments. What was a white-throated sparrow doing in Kentucky in the summer? And how did a canyon wren end up in Michigan? The birders were horrified.

The lesson? Don't fudge the truth before a large audience. A little white lie that might go unnoticed in an e-mail to one person could be a real embarrassment in a mass mailing or on a bulletin board read by hundreds of people.

Stretching the truth isn't the only thing that can get you in trouble with a big audience. Be careful about using irony or humor, especially with people you know only in the virtual world. You'd be surprised how easy it is for someone to take your words the wrong way. And don't sound off on sensitive subjects like politics or religion or sex, unless you're willing to take some flak. The larger the audience, the more likely you are to touch a sore spot.

You can never know for sure who'll read your electronic writing. Even a note to a few friends may be forwarded to a few more and a few more. Before you know it, that one-liner about deconstructionism may end up in Jacques Derrida's mailbox. Of course, that may be exactly where you want it.

Our editor, Jane, sent a friend an e-mail with a joke about the trials and tribulations of undergoing a mammogram. (We'll spare you the details.) The friend sent it on to Pat Schroeder, the former congresswoman, who then forwarded it to all the women in Congress, urging them to send it to their gynecologists and radiologists as a lesson in awareness. How's that for getting the word out?

You Are What You Write

In real life, chatting up strangers is harder for some than it is for others. But in the online world, the shy guy is often Mr. Personality. He thrives amid the anonymity, the attitude that cyberspace is an embarrassment-free zone where wallflowers can jump right in. At the computer he can be himself, accepted for who he is.

True, the Internet is the ultimate in democracy, one of the great levelers of our time. Bulletin boards, chat rooms, and newsgroups are an equal-opportunity bunch. Unless you tell them, people won't know your age, your religion, your skin color, your social status, how good-looking you are, how big your bank account is, where you live, what you're wearing (or not wearing), what you do for a living, whether you speak with an accent, whether your roots need touching up, whether you're writing from an office chair or a wheelchair or the cab of a pickup truck.

Many people think this anonymity makes good writing unnecessary. Who cares how you write if nobody knows who you are? Yet the fact that people don't know you makes the quality of your writing all the more important. If you're a lousy writer, you have no control over how you and your message come across. Online, you're judged solely by what you write—not by your ideas alone, but by how you express them.

So relax and be yourself on the Internet. Enjoy the feeling of liberation. Just don't lose sight of the fact that in the virtual world, the real you is what you write.

5. A Click and a Promise
Getting the Facts Straight

Steve, a screenwriter we know, was asked to appear in a chat room at a film festival in Florida. He was scheduled to go on right after a teen movie goddess, but her flight was delayed and her online fans were growing restless. Hey, Steve thought, the show must go on, right? So, with a wink from the host, he went on for her—not just *for* her, but *as* her.

Steve, who makes his living bringing fantasies to life, managed to pull it off. He knew just enough about the subject—the young actress, the buzz about her latest movie, the glam Hollywood scene—to convince her fans she was there in the studio.

No one's saying you should go into a chat room and pose as the celeb of the moment. But if you want to be believable when you write online, learn as much as you can about your subject. E-mail is such a snap that people often reach for the mouse before checking their facts. They care more about speed than accuracy. Imagine this scenario:

It's a Friday afternoon in August and Sue Ann is dying to get off the "Happy Homemaker" set. At last the coast is clear. The pots and pans have been put away, the stacks of recipes filed, and the philodendron watered. Everything that needs attention has been dealt with, disposed of, or dumped on Mary. Then, as she's almost out the door, Sue Ann hears that electronic flourish that says she has mail.

Back to the old terminal. Whew! She's in luck. It's just one of those "Have a nice weekend" dispatches from Georgette. By the way, Georgette adds, she's planning a mushroom-hunting expedition and can't remember whether the poisonous ones have orange stripes or purple spots. Does the Happy Homemaker happen to know?

Luckily, this won't take long, e-mail being so breezy and casual and all. Sue Ann clicks Reply and types: "Purple spots. Have fungi. LOL."

Smiling at her clever pun, Sue Ann heads for the elevator. Halfway home, she starts to wonder. Did Georgette ask which were edible, or which were poisonous? Oh well, it's only e-mail. (*Cue ominous music.*)

The Misinformation Highway

The other day we rented a video of the movie *Desk Set,* with Katharine Hepburn, Dina Merrill, and Joan Blondell as fact-checkers at a TV network in the fifties. Spencer Tracy, the efficiency expert, comes along and wants to computerize the research department. Things go haywire, naturally. Automation, it seems, is no substitute for the human touch.

We've come a long way since the computer was the size of a school gym, but we still haven't created a program that can fact-check as well as Kate and company. Never mind all that information in cyberspace and all the computing power on our desks. We still need a human brain to separate the facts from the fluff.

Where information is concerned, never tell yourself "It's only e-mail" or "It's only a Web page" or "It's only a newsgroup." The truth is the truth, in the virtual world as well as the real one. Know what you're writing about before you write about it. Don't expect the computer to know the subject for you.

Everyone makes mistakes, of course. You can get away with one here or there, but if the screw-ups accumulate, you'll get a reputation for spouting misinformation. We're not talking about deliberate lies, only the everyday blunders you make when you're in a hurry.

People lose their inhibitions online and become careless. They view the virtual world as international waters, where anything goes, even a leaky boat with a captain who doesn't know the way. They take for granted what comes easily, and not much is easier than clicking Reply, banging out a few dozen words, and hitting Send. Somehow, knowing what they're talking about seems less important online. After all, it's not as if they were putting something on paper, signing it, and sending it through the U.S. Postal Service.

Okay, no one expects an e-mail to look like a formal letter. It's usually shorter, more casual, and written in more of a hurry, like a quickie note or a postcard. But brevity, informality, and speed don't excuse fudging the facts. And incidentally, getting the facts right means getting the math right. (For more on numbers, see chapter 9.)

If you don't know your subject, nothing else matters. Your grammar may be great, your spelling beyond reproach, your figures of speech perfect tens. But who cares when there's no *there* there?

Don't hit Send until you have the facts straight. What you don't know, you can learn. What you're not sure of, you can check. What's uncheckable should be labeled as such. Put yourself in the reader's place and write the kind of message you'd like to get, one you can trust.

The Uncertainty Principle

You've probably heard about the college student who made a killing in the market by planting a phony press release on an Internet news wire. He wiped out half the value of a high-tech company's shares in minutes. Panicky investors sold at a loss before the stock rebounded.

Most of us don't set out to mislead anybody. If we pass on incorrect information, it's probably because we don't have the time or the resources to check our facts.

In the best of all possible worlds, everyone would know everything he had to know when he sat down at the keyboard to write. But let's get real. What does a guy do when he *thinks* he's right but can't honestly say he *knows* he is?

Sure, he could wait until he's absolutely, positively, categorically certain (though by then he'll have forgotten why he was looking up the item in the first place). Here's a novel idea: After making a reasonable effort to check, he could clearly identify what he *knows,* what he *thinks,* what he *hears,* and so on. That way, the reader can tell the positivelys from the maybes.

Almost everybody who writes online believes he's an expert, so it's hard to admit when you don't know something. But give it a try. Honesty isn't just responsible. It's refreshing! Who knows? You might even start a movement.

Fast Forward

Perhaps you were among the lucky ones who received a promotional e-mail from Victoria Johnson, founder of Victoria's Secret, offering a $50 gift certificate for forwarding the message to nine friends. Guess what? There is no Victoria. And the company, founded by a guy named Roy, is now owned by a Fortune 500 corporation that doesn't need you to help sell its sexy lingerie. Sorry.

Even people who are meticulous about the facts in their own writing may be careless about forwarding someone else's. When a goodie comes their way online, they'll simply hit Forward and forget about it. If you don't want your friends taken in by online humbug, however, check out whatever you forward to them. Don't have the time? Say so. Or better still, don't forward what you can't vouch for.

And if you're one of the people who sent Vickie's e-mail to nine of your friends, go to the blackboard and write this fifty times: "When something online sounds too good to be true, it probably is." (For more about chain letters, see chapter 3.)

The Sum of Its Ports

In our corner of Connecticut, the local paper reported that a rural Jewish congregation had found a new Bible scroll by clicking on the search engine Ask Jeeves and inquiring, "Where can I buy a Sefer Torah?" Is that divine inspiration or what?

As anybody with a functioning temporal lobe has heard, you can find all kinds of goods and services on the Web, from shrinks to shrunken heads. A woman in upstate New York even used the Internet to find a surgeon in Houston who removed her damaged heart, fixed it, and put it back in her chest.

When you're trying to learn more about a subject, there's almost no limit to the information available in cyberspace. Unfortunately, much of it is unreliable. The virtual world is a vast wilderness of misinformation, exaggeration, half-baked theories, crackpot prognostications, undependable estimates, wacko statistics, and outright lies.

This doesn't mean you should avoid using the Web, bulletin boards, mailing lists, and the rest of the Internet to gather facts. Just be certain they're facts before you put them in your online writing.

You might begin by going to one of the Web sites devoted to debunking the many myths making the rounds in cyberspace. Search for "Internet myths" or "urban legends" and you'll never again be so trusting of what you read online.

A few of the pseudo-facts you can find on the Internet without really trying: Mel Gibson's face is a re-construction. A big American bank has cyanide-laced glue on its deposit envelopes. Marilyn Monroe had six toes on one foot. Donkeys kill more people annually than plane crashes. Coconut milk can be substituted for blood plasma. (In prehistoric times, when we were in high school, one popular myth was that beehive hairdos were favorite nesting places for spiders. That one managed to sweep the country without benefit of the Internet.)

How can you tell good info from bad? Be skeptical. Assume that online information is guilty until proven innocent. To start with, consider the source. If we were checking out the title of a P. G. Wodehouse novel, we'd give more weight to the Library of Congress's Web site than to Earl and Bonnie's home page.

But even blue-chip sites may have inaccurate or outdated information. The online *Encyclopaedia Britannica,* for one, had bad data, later corrected, about a type of cancer. If you have time, check your material with two or three solid sources. If you can't verify it, at least say where the info came from and perhaps add a hyperlink so the reader can judge for himself.

The Little Engine That Could

People waste hours online looking for information they could have found in minutes at the local library. Here are some tricks to speed up your computer searches:

1. Ask friends for their favorite search engines, try them out, and use the ones that work best for you. But don't get in a rut. New engines are always popping up, and today's hot number may be lukewarm in six months.

2. Take time to read the "Search Tips" for each engine you use (no, engines aren't all alike). Ten or fifteen minutes spent now can save hours later. For example, most search engines will find exact phrases if you put them in quotation marks.

3. Spell your search words correctly. Say you're doing research on *The Thin Man*. The pickings will be slim if you misspell "Dashiell Hammett."

4. Use unusual search words. Perhaps you need to know the plot of *Sir Harry Hotspur of Humblethwaite*. If you search for "Trollope" or "Trollope novel," you'll get thousands of hits. Even a search for "Sir Harry Hotspur" could turn up a bunch of irrelevant sites (including one for an English soccer team called the Hotspurs and named after a different Sir Harry). But a search for "Humblethwaite" will do the trick faster than you can say "Plantagenet Palliser."

5. Stay focused. Don't be distracted by sites that are fascinating yet beside the point. (Obvious advice, but hard to follow.)

Cheating Hearts

Come September, days grow shorter, birds begin to migrate, and wired high school seniors discover a college-admissions essay on the Web by a well-rounded guy who writes operas, builds bridges, plays bluegrass cello, and bakes thirty-minute brownies in twenty minutes. A few students with more chutzpah than originality will hit Select All and send copies of the humorous spoof to prospective colleges as their own work.

Bad move. Admissions officers around the country are familiar with the facetious essay (the author also raises clams, plays Hamlet, fights bulls, spies for the CIA) and automatically disqualify any applicant who plagiarizes it.

Cheating is nothing new. Students have passed off other people's work as their own—and been caught—since way back when. But things have gotten out of hand lately, thanks to the Internet. Why bother with tiresome research, fact-checking, and writing when you can simply cut and paste somebody else's work with a few keystrokes?

And if that's too much trouble, there are Web sites that will do the cutting and pasting for you. Suppose you want a biology term paper on the detoxification of xenobiotics by plant cells. Or one for law school on substantive due process. Or perhaps a paper for twentieth-century lit on death and duality in Virginia Woolf's *Mrs. Dalloway.* You can go to a Web site like lazystudents.com, cheaters.com, or geniuspapers.com and download a ready-made paper for so much a page. A custom job will cost you more.

No money? Countless other sites offer free papers on everything from abdominoplasty to Kwanzaa, onychophorans to zydeco. Where's the catch?

Well, the Web has some terrific stuff, but much of what passes for information—the free as well as the pricey—is often misinformation. In the time it would take you to check out the facts in that book report you want to steal, you could write your own. If that doesn't persuade you to go straight, consider this.

Teachers at colleges and universities across the country are now using cheat-catching software to compare homework with all that good, and not so good, material available on the Web. So the whiz-bang essay you were sure was worth an A may get you an F, if it doesn't get you expelled.

Even if you pull it off (here comes the sermon), the person you're cheating is you. You may never again need to know about xenobiotics or onychophorans. But you will need to write. And you learn how by doing your own writing, not by downloading somebody else's. In the age of the computer, anybody who can't write can't connect.

PART II

Alpha Mail

6. Natural Selection
Conciser Is Nicer

In the age of the Internet, we're told, people and their machines are cranking out more information every year or so than they did in all of pre-digital history. No wonder we're suffering from information overload.

Much of the overload, as it happens, is information about how to cope with information overload. You can even find software programs to summarize or highlight those wordy e-mails and Web pages and downloads and attachments. If only they worked.

We tested one by feeding it the opening lines of *Pride and Prejudice.* This is how Jane Austen's witty comments on matrimony were summed up: "Wife, fortune, possession, daughters, rightful property, surrounding families, minds." Indeed! You'd be better off with a Classics Illustrated comic book.

Why are computer users grasping at anything— even ineffective software—to lighten the load? More important, why should they have to? One big reason is that too many people are writing too much about too many things.

The computer has made it easy to write and hard to stop. Picture yourself at the keyboard. Fingers fly faster than thought. Words tumble upon words. When you run out of your own words, you can cut and paste somebody else's. And never mind the astronomical word count. You'll trim later, naturally, if you have the time.

In the old days (remember typewriters? carbon copies?), writing was harder. When you made a mistake, you had to do a whole page over again—or be an artist with the correction fluid. Chances are, you thought before you wrote. You sorted your ideas. You considered, perhaps, four or five possible ways of saying something, then chose the best one. Maybe you even scribbled things out first on a yellow pad.

Today, you dump every version into your word processor. If you can't decide which is best, you keep them all. Then some poor reader has to slog through four or five paragraphs when one would have been enough.

What should you do about it? You might go to your brokers' Web site and buy stock in data-storage companies. Or you could try to cut down on the data by saying what you have to say—enough and no more—when you write online.

Many people think the way to save words in an e-mail is to ditch salutations and signatures, on the theory that computer-generated addresses do the job. We disagree. A "Hi, Lois" and a "See you, Clark" can give e-mail a human touch and make it easier on the eye. There are better places to cut, as you'll see.

Initial Public Offering

We were poking around in a used-book store one day and found a real piece of Americana, a 1917 writing guide called *Fifteen Thousand Useful Phrases.* We won't list all 15,000, but among them were these suggestions for beginning a business letter:

"We beg a moment of your attention and serious consideration..."

"We desire to express our appreciation of your patronage..."

"We acknowledge with pleasure the receipt of your order..."

"You will find interest, we believe, in this advance announcement..."

Business writing has come a long way since then, right? Wrong. Our friend Ann was opening a stack of mail at her office recently and discovered an earth-shaking bulletin that began: "This courtesy letter precedes my intention to call you." (Wouldn't a simple "I'll be calling you about..." have been better?)

Empty openings are bad enough in "real" letters, but they can be deal-breakers in e-mail. The wired reader has a short attention span, and it becomes shorter as the queue in her electronic mailbox becomes longer. She has little tolerance for meaningless throat-clearing. Put a lot of nothing at the beginning and she may delete your message before reaching the nitty-gritty.

Don't try her patience. Get to the point.

These are the sorts of beginnings that make readers nod off in their ergonomic chairs:

> *I'd like to take up just a few moments of your time, if I may, to acquaint you with the ophthalmological benefits of our new 3-D monitors.* (Better: *If eyestrain is a problem in your office, our new 3-D monitors may be the answer.*)

> *I've been too busy to answer my e-mail lately, but in the process of catching up on some of it I found your message about the rubber plant that's missing from the lobby.* (If you're so busy, get on with it: *Thanks for alerting me about the missing rubber plant.*)

> *I don't know whether this will come as a surprise or not, but you've been chosen to represent the boogie-board division at the sales conference in Honolulu.* (Skip the preliminaries and let's boogie: *You've been chosen to represent the boogie-board division at the sales conference in Honolulu.*)

> *After carefully reviewing the latest research on the antidepressant effects of chocolate, we have concluded that our serotonin reuptake inhibitor is*

more effective than a Hershey bar and it won't raise cholesterol levels. (Raise your reader's spirits by putting the news first: *Our serotonin reuptake inhibitor is more effective than a Hershey bar at fighting depression and it won't raise cholesterol levels, according to the latest research.*)

Now seems as good a time as any to sound out the R&D people about an issue that I've been meaning to mention but never got around to. (So get to it.)

A report to shareholders is probably not the best place to discuss the ups and downs of our long effort to develop an edible microchip, so let's go straight to how things stand now. (Drop that sentence and go straight to the status quo.)

No doubt you're wondering why I'm e-mailing you about the Snapple machine when we just discussed it, but under the circumstances a follow-up contact might be in order. (Make it snappy: *The Snapple machine is broken again.*)

By this time, you must be tired of hearing people say that your presentation yesterday would have been more effective if your fly had been zipped. (Tell him something he hasn't heard.)

Getting down to business doesn't mean being abrupt or rude or bossy. A few well-chosen words can make the difference between a demand and a request. Instead of "Get me the report by 2:30," try "I'd like the report by 2:30." A "please" now and then won't kill you, either.

And now, to finish with beginnings. If you're replying to a message, remind the reader what the message was. "Great idea" isn't good enough when you're answering someone who sends scores of e-mails every day. What great idea?

Many an e-mail is thrown away because it has a throwaway beginning, so look twice at your opening sentence. If it's deletable, delete it.

Downsizing

If you have a baby and a spare computer at home, you may be familiar with KeyWack, a software program that lets infants produce funny sounds and pictures by whacking away at the keyboard. Grown-ups, too, sometimes hit the keys thoughtlessly, but the result isn't so entertaining—unless you're amused by irrelevant, redundant, interminable writing.

The less time you spend thinking about your message, the more time someone else has to spend reading it. This isn't a particularly new observation. The French philosopher Blaise Pascal (there's a computer language named for him) suggested much the same thing in a note to a friend a few hundred years ago: "I have made this longer than usual, only because I have not had the time to make it shorter."

Writing more is easy. Writing less takes effort. But it's worth the effort. Everyone online knows that short messages are read first and long ones are saved for later (if they're read at all).

"No one reads long e-mails!" says Kate, a friend who works for a big online bookstore. "If you can't keep it to a screenful, forget it."

Obviously, you can't—and shouldn't—hold every e-mail to a screenful. If you're writing to a loved one who cherishes your every word, more is better. If you're writing to a friend who can't get enough juicy gossip, by all means put in every delicious tidbit. If you're writing a business message that requires tact—say, a memo announcing that the company is in deep doo-doo—a few extra words can make all the difference.

But in general, Kate is right. Shorter is better, especially at the office. A reader should be able to tell at a glance who you are (if necessary), why you're writing, and how urgent your message is. Does it have to be answered right away? Can it wait until tomorrow (or next week)? Can it be delegated to someone else?

When you reply to an e-mail, there's no need to copy the entire message in your response. A simple reminder is usually enough: *Your suggestion about the mouse in the cafeteria is brilliant. I sent it on to Grizabella and she'll get back to you about it.* If you do copy, repeat only the relevant parts, and no more.

Sometimes people reply more often than they have to. Jean, a psychologist, was making her way through the eighty-four e-mails that had piled up in her in-basket when a virtual lightbulb went on over her head. She could save time and write less by reading all the incoming messages on the same subject (or from the same person) before answering. Maybe a problem raised in one e-mail was resolved in a later one. A plan mentioned in one might have been altered by another farther down in the queue. Perhaps a fuzzy idea had evolved over several e-mails into a clear proposal that could be handled in one simple response.

If you're the methodical type, you'll find it hard not to check off those accumulated e-mails one by one. But don't plunge in. The best time to begin trimming is before you begin writing.

How else can you say more with less?

- Say it once. You might come up with three terrific ways to say something, but an e-mail or other online message isn't the place for all three.
- Cut and paste only what you need. If you want to pass on one recipe from a long article on Tex-Mex cuisine, don't send the whole enchilada.
- Get rid of redundant phrases. Instead of calling someone *tall of stature,* simply say he's *tall.* Instead of *pretty in appearance,* or *green in color,* or *smooth to the touch,* why not just *pretty,* or *green,* or *smooth?*
- Don't make two words do the job of one. A *true fact* is just a fact. A *foreign import* is only an import. An *advance plan* is still a plan. If someone's *personally responsible,* she's simply responsible.

- Be sparing with the stuffing. If an expression like *sort of, kind of, really, very, a bit, a little, actually, rather,* or *somewhat* is merely taking up space, drop it. But don't go too far. An occasional *really* or *rather* or *very* can help loosen up a stiff message. (See more about empty expressions in chapter 7.)

Dave, a newspaperman who's plagued by windy e-mail, wishes his software could cut off a rambling message the way his telephone answering machine hangs up after a minute. "All right already!" he says.

But when is enough enough? How can you tell it's time to stop writing and hit Send? We got an idea from our friend Deb, whose law firm bills by the tenth of an hour. She reminds clients who e-mail her that they can save money by making every word count. So what we do when we go online is imagine we're e-mailing our lawyer and the meter is running.

Point Counter Point

In the PowerPoint management style, you can reduce anything to a few slides with heaps of bullets, charts, and color-block graphics. But anybody who's sat through one too many PowerPoint presentations knows you can dumb something down until there's nothing left.

We love a spoof we found on the Web. A computer scientist who'd had his fill of mind-numbing visual aids came up with a PowerPoint version of Lincoln's Gettysburg Address. Our favorite slide is headed "REVIEW OF KEY OBJECTIVES & CRITICAL SUCCESS FACTORS," and its final bulleted item reads: "Gov't of/by/for the people." So much for eloquence. (As a Clemson University professor lamented to a friend of ours, "In the age of PowerPoint, the five-paragraph essay is being replaced by a title card and three bullets.")

What's the point of all this? First, simple is good, but minimalism has its limits. Second, oversimplified visual aids can obscure an idea instead of enhancing it. And third, if you explain something clearly, you can skip the slide show.

7. The E-Mail Eunuch
Beefing Up Wussy Writing

Some people don't just write *on* computers. They write *for* them. Future MBA's, for instance. If you applied to business school in recent years, a computer program called e-rater helped grade the essays you wrote for the Graduate Management Admission Test.

Machines, it turns out, aren't hard to please. You don't have to write clearly or powerfully or stylishly to knock e-rater's socks off. All you have to do is write a lot (that shows you know a lot), and throw in complicated sentences (you must be smart), tons of synonyms (what a big vocabulary!), and plenty of words like "meanwhile," "therefore," "for example," and "since" (signs of a tidy mind).

No need to sweat over creativity, subtlety, individuality, and style—the things a real reader looks for in writing. As far as e-rater is concerned, they don't compute. This doesn't seem to bother the Educational Testing Service, which developed the software. "Unlike human scorers," the ETS has said on its Web site, "computers are not subject to fatigue, and their scoring is not colored by previous life experiences."

We can't argue with that. But if you're writing to people who *are* subject to fatigue and who *have* experienced life, act accordingly. Be clear, direct, active, colorful, original, and most of all, simple. That doesn't mean simpleminded. Any idiot can be incomprehensible. You have to know something to explain it in plain English.

Some puffed-up writers use long words, techie talk, trendy terms, and convoluted sentences to cover up or deceive or sound important or go along with the crowd. Most people who inflate their writing, though, are simply insecure, often for no good reason. They don't feel their ideas are strong enough, and they prop them up with elaborate language.

If your ideas are any good, they can stand on their own. So kick away those unnecessary props. All they do is turn a strong writer into a wuss.

Great Affectations

Stewart was tooling along the info highway, listening to all-news radio on Real Audio, when he caught an ad for "pre-need memorial property." Death, where is thy sting?

Something strange is going on out there, and not just with cemetery plots. People are standing on their heads to avoid using plain English. A summary is "a top-level repositioning of what was learned." Aloof

bosses are "hierarchically siloed paradigm managers."
People aren't fired—they're "deselected," "down-
sized," "outplaced," "redeployed," "separated," "tran-
sitioned," or "prematurely retired."

When you go through contortions to sound authoritative, avoid unpleasantness, or pull a fast one,
you usually don't fool anyone—not for long, anyway.
In the end, you only make things worse.

We're all tempted to use pretentious or round-
about language at one time or another. Why? It's easier than saying something clearly. You have to know
your subject to be clear. Besides, big words are so
damned impressive, especially when the reader doesn't
know what they mean. Who cares if you're not understood, as long as you look good? And for those
who practice to deceive, convoluted language is the
next best thing to a lie.

If what you want to do is communicate, not impress or mislead, keep it simple. When you mean acid
rain, don't say "atmospheric deposition of anthro-
pogenically derived acidic substances." An explosion
is an explosion, not an "unplanned rapid ignition."
And an "intrusion detection device" won't stop a
prowler any better than a burglar alarm. But it might
stop a reader, especially an online reader.

Nobody should have to translate your e-mail.
Steer clear of vague, hyped-up, needlessly technical
language and say what you mean. Here's what to
avoid:

- **Oversized Words.** Try not to use a big word if a short one works better. "Snow" is not only shorter but says more than "inclement weather" (which could mean rain, fog, or gale-force winds). There's nothing wrong with using a long word when you need one, but short words are often more efficient. If you don't have the tools to solve a problem right away, for example, don't make it worse by saying: *An optimal finalization cannot be facilitated in the immediate time frame because the enabling mechanisms were negatively impacted.* Rely on the strength of your ideas, not the length of your words.

- **Jargon.** Stay away from bureaucratic or technical language that may be gobbledygook to your reader. Insider words that are handy among colleagues can be meaningless to outsiders. If you're a doctor e-mailing another doctor, "inflamed periungual tissue" is fine, but if you're e-mailing a patient, go with "hangnail." As for you techies, save the computerese for other techies. The rest of us get enough double-talk from our computers without getting it from Tech Support, too. Consider your audience.

- **Trendy Words.** Fashions come and go, and what's in today may be out tomorrow (or mean nothing at all). If you expect your online writing to be around for a while—on a Web page, maybe, or in an e-mail with staying power—avoid language with a sell-by date. That includes "sell-by date."

- **Foreign Terms.** There's a certain *je ne sais quoi* about foreign phrases. (*Je ne sais quoi* is a good example. It's a classy way of saying you don't know.) For the most part, if you're writing in English, stick to English. That doesn't mean you can't use foreign words now and then. English, after all, has been absorbing them for centuries. But take it easy. If you go on *ad nauseam,* you'll sound like a show-off. *Capisc'?*

- **Euphemisms.** Anyone who's searched the real estate ads for a place to live knows what a euphemism is. "Cozy" and "intimate" are buzzwords for small. "Full of character" means it's a dump. "Great potential" is practically hopeless. "Spacious and airy" is another way of saying drafty and impossible to heat. "Original details" is code for get a good contractor. Sugarcoating may help a pill go down easier, but it makes a writer look dishonest. So hold the hype.

- **Pseudoscientific Terms.** Quick! Define "parameter." Having trouble? We're not surprised. Every time we see the word, it means something else: a characteristic, a variable, an element, a part, a component, a boundary, a quality, a requirement, a feature, an ingredient, a perimeter, and so on. In fact, "parameter" means so many things that it means nothing. Two other authoritative-sounding words, "paradigm" and "dynamic," are almost as hard to define. Don't use pseudoscientific terms that are tough to pin down: *The parameters of our solution comprised a paradigm of the problem-solving dynamic.* Translation: *Our solution was a good example of problem solving.*

Simple writing isn't just short, straight, familiar, and honest. It's also eloquent. Over the years, the two of us have read about as much as it's possible to read and still live a normal life. What we've found is that the best writing—the writing that means the most and stays with us the longest—is the simplest.

Wipe that doubtful look off your face. Pick up a great book—*Emma, Huckleberry Finn, Animal Farm, Mrs. Dalloway, Catch-22, The Power and the Glory.* See how straightforward it is? Time after time, you'll find that the deeper the thought, the plainer the language. The more beautiful the writing, the simpler the words.

"When You Are Old," by William Butler Yeats, is one of the most beautiful poems in English. Yet it couldn't be any simpler. This is how it begins:

> *When you are old and grey and full of sleep,*
> *And nodding by the fire, take down this book,*
> *And slowly read, and dream of the soft look*
> *Your eyes had once, and of their shadows deep...*

Never underestimate the power of one-syllable words. They're good enough for great literature, and they're good enough for e-mail.

Clarity Begins at Home

"If I seem unduly clear to you," Alan Greenspan once joked to Congress, "you must have misunderstood what I said." What he meant was that Fed chairmen have to be masters of obscurity. Plain talk has a way of sending the stock market into a tailspin.

The rest of us don't have to worry about moving the market. We'd rather be understood. For us, there's no such thing as too much clarity in our online writing. Unfortunately, an idea that's crystal clear to the sender isn't always so clear to the reader.

Don't assume anything. If a message can be screwed up, it will be. Take responsibility for your writing and accept that any misinterpretation is your fault, not the reader's. There are many ways to make an e-mail or other online message easier to follow.

- Divide long sentences into shorter ones. Nothing is more irritating to a reader than getting lost halfway through a sentence and having to start over again. He may not bother.
- Break the message into paragraphs. A huge block of uninterrupted type makes a reader's eyes roll back in her head. Split it into short paragraphs with one topic per paragraph. You might even leave a little white space in between.
- Use the right connections. Words and phrases like *also, although, at any rate, because, but,* and *however* connect our ideas. Without connections, these ideas

don't fit together: *Lady Eustace seldom wears her diamonds, they're insured for a fortune.* What's missing? A connection: *Lady Eustace seldom wears her diamonds,* **even though** *they're insured for a fortune.* Some connecting words can be tricky, however— and that includes *however.* This sentence doesn't work: *Lady Eustace seldom wears her diamonds,* **however,** *they're insured for a fortune.* We can't tell whether *however* is attached to the first part or the second. It might mean this: *Lady Eustace seldom wears her diamonds.* **However,** *they're insured for a fortune.* Or this: *Lady Eustace seldom wears her diamonds,* **however.** *They're insured for a fortune.*

- Check *it* out. Little words like *it, he, she,* and *they* are handy for replacing long words or phrases (like "creamed chipped beef on toast," "Wittgenstein," "Dr. Joyce Brothers," and "the wives of Henry VIII"). But these stand-ins work only when the reader knows what's being replaced. Here's an example of an unidentified flying *it: Harry was using his laptop to track Springer Motors' stock on a flight from Wilmington to Detroit when* **it** *crashed.* What crashed? The laptop? The stock? The flight? Reboot the sentence, perhaps like this: *Harry's laptop crashed when he was using* **it** *to track Springer Motors' stock on a flight from Wilmington to Detroit.*

- Be clear about time and place. You may know when and where something happened (or will happen), but your reader doesn't. And this kind of sentence is no help: *Mel decided to write a new scene for Roger De Bris in Chicago Thursday.* Is Chicago where Mel made the decision or where he'll write the scene? Is Thursday when he decided this or when he'll do the writing? Here's one possibility: *Mel decided Thursday in Chicago to write a new scene for Roger De Bris.*

- Give good directions. Words that tell us where we are (such as *about, before, on,* and *over*) can sometimes be read two ways. *Agatha's lecture on the Orient-Express* could be aboard the train or about it. *A dispute over Hillary's office* could mean a squabble about it or above it. *Radiohead's appearance before the Mormon Tabernacle Choir* could mean the band is performing for the choir or ahead of it.

Sending an e-mail that's unclear is like mumbling to an answering machine. Try not to leave a message that could be misinterpreted. And good grammar never hurts, either.

Disorderly Conduct

While driving home from a trip to Cape Cod, our friends Ann and David stopped for a snack at an eatery in Rhode Island. This tasty morsel was on the menu: "Customers who are especially vulnerable to food borne illness should order and eat food from animals thoroughly cooked or pasteurized."

Why do we imagine a Hereford in a hot tub? According to the menu, the livestock should be cooked or pasteurized, not the food that comes from it. The sentence is clumsy because the parts are out of order. Something (*from animals*) has come between two ideas that ought to be directly connected (*food* and *thoroughly cooked or pasteurized*).

Disorderly writing isn't limited to restaurant menus. The ideas in online messages also get out of line. Here's an example of two parts that don't quite go together: *Scrolling through my address book, your name jumped out at me.* Come again? Who's doing the scrolling here, the e-mailer or a name in the address book? As it stands, the first part of the sentence (*Scrolling through my address book*) is attached to *your name,* not to the sender. Let's put the sender into the picture: *As I was scrolling through my address book, your name jumped out at me.* Or: *Your name jumped out at me as I was scrolling through my address book.*

You can pack a lot of ideas into a sentence if they're in order. One misplaced idea can lead to confusing, embarrassing, and clumsy writing. Luckily, it's not that difficult to keep your ideas straight.

• Put the subject and verb as close together as possible. The minimum requirement for a sentence — even a tiny one like *Atlas shrugged* — is a subject (*Atlas*) and a verb (*shrugged*). You can add all the information you want, as long as you keep the subject (the actor) close to the verb (the action). If you put too much between them, you get something like this: *Atlas, finding the problems of the world too heavy for his shoulders, shrugged.* Now let's bring the subject and verb together: *Finding the problems of the world too heavy for his shoulders, Atlas shrugged.* Isn't that easier to read?

- Put descriptive words close to what they describe. If you separate them, you may confuse your readers. A case in point: *The Beardstown ladies regretted investing in the start-up deeply.* Did the ladies deeply regret, or did they deeply invest? You can clear up the confusion by putting the descriptive word (*deeply*) next to the word it belongs with. You might mean this: *The Beardstown ladies deeply regretted investing in the start-up.* Or this: *The Beardstown ladies regretted investing deeply in the start-up.*

- Put descriptive phrases next to what they describe. Here's one that got away: *As a value investor, the high-flying technology sector didn't interest Warren.* What or who was the value investor—the tech sector, or Warren? Let's put the descriptive phrase (*As a value investor*) next to the guy being described: *As a value investor, Warren wasn't interested in the high-flying technology sector.*

When the parts of a sentence get out of order, mismatches are inevitable. The trick to avoiding them is no trick at all—just go directly from point to point, idea to idea, with no detours along the way. Give the reader one idea at a time.

Enter Active

Let's say your Subaru got into a heated discussion with a Chevy Suburban in the parking lot at the mall and the Suburban won. Now it's time to break the bad news to your significant other. Will you be a man and fess up (*I totaled the car, dear*)? Or a wuss who won't take the fall (*Dear, the car has been totaled*)?

The backward, or passive, writer (our friend the wuss) plays a shell game with the subject of a sentence. He switches the usual order of things—subject (*I*), verb (*totaled*), object (*the car*)—and hides the "real" subject.

Using a passive verb (*The car has been totaled*) instead of an active one (*I totaled the car*) is saying what was done but not whodunit. This can be a handy way to avoid identifying the culprit, whether the guilty party is you or somebody else. A defense attorney, for one, might use the passive in an appeal for leniency: *The Subaru was totaled.* Not: *My client totaled the Subaru.*

Public figures often use passive verbs when they don't want to be held accountable for their words. A politician who's weaseling out of a promise not to run for a third term might say: *A pledge was made but it's not considered binding.* Not: *I made a pledge but I don't consider it binding.* A CEO who predicted a ten-percent rise in earnings and now has to explain a twenty-percent drop might say: *The projection was understated because the changing market could not have been anticipated.* Not: *I understated the projection because I didn't anticipate the changing market.*

Many scientists and academics have convinced themselves that passive writing is objective writing. They think phrases like "it is believed" or "it is understood" are somehow more legitimate than "I believe" or "I understand." Well, don't you believe it. If you have the facts, why weaken them with wimpy writing? People who want to disguise their ignorance go for passive verbs: *It is indicated that additional research is required before a clear understanding of this phenomenon can be reached.* Translation: *I don't have a clue.*

We're not saying you should never use a passive verb. There are times when you may want to back into a sentence. Maybe it doesn't matter who did it: *The earthquake damage will be appraised next week.* (Instead of: *The insurance company will appraise the earthquake damage next week.*) Or say you want to save a surprise for the end: *During the aftershock, Nicholas was beaned on the head by a Fabergé egg.* (Instead of: *A Fabergé egg beaned Nicholas on the head during the aftershock.*) Or perhaps you'd like to soften a blow: *Our earthquake insurance was allowed to lapse, honey.* (Instead of: *You allowed our earthquake insurance to lapse, Nicholas.*)

You may also prefer to leave out the responsible party in cases like these:

- You don't know: *My Harley-Davidson Barbie was stolen.*
- You don't care: *Three suspects were questioned.*
- You don't want to say: *I was given a peek at their rap sheets.*

But those are exceptions. Go for active verbs whenever you can. Active writers are responsible writers. Besides, they're usually easier to read.

Hyper Text

We love getting e-mail from a friend of ours in Minneapolis. When we see Dimi's address in the mailbox, we know we're in for a treat. She doesn't just "get" tickets to the NCAA Final Four—she "scores" them. Her vacation plans aren't "uncertain"—they're "scrambled." She doesn't "have" visitors—she "survives" them. And the big chiefs in her company don't "meet"—they "powwow."

We'd look forward to hearing from Dimi even if her writing were as bland as an airline meal. But we read her messages before many others because of the colorful and interesting words she uses.

Writing that's interesting isn't necessarily weird or unusual or even original. It may simply use familiar words in unexpected ways. If you'd like to make your online vocabulary more lively and colorful, keep these ideas in mind:

- A verb is better than a noun. The verb has more

electricity because it's where the action is. So look for ways to replace nouns with verbs. Wimpy: *The composition of the ballet's music took Igor only two weeks.* Better: *Igor composed the ballet's music in only two weeks.*

- A strong verb is better than a weak one. English is packed with powerful verbs. If yours isn't doing much work, find a better one. Wimpy: *Tragedy occurred on opening night, when Tatiana performed a pirouette and sustained a broken toe.* Better: *Tragedy struck on opening night, when Tatiana pirouetted and broke a toe.*

- A strong verb doesn't need an adverb. If a verb has to be propped up, replace it. Wimpy: *Sergei quickly went to help the fallen ballerina.* Better: *Sergei rushed to help the fallen ballerina.* Adverbs (words that describe or modify verbs) are symptoms of weak writing.

- A strong adjective can energize a weak noun. Through no fault of their own, nouns (words for people, places, or things) sometimes need help. That's where adjectives (words that describe or modify nouns) come in. Take this adjective-free sentence: *The understudy laced up her tutu as the ballerina was carried offstage.* Now notice how a couple of adjectives add drama to the scene: *The ambitious understudy laced up her tutu as the ashen ballerina was carried offstage.* But don't overdo it: *The ambitious, scheming, manipulative understudy smirked at the corps de ballet.* Sometimes one adjective can take the place of several words. Wimpy: *Hours after her triumph, she fell into a* **manhole that had been left open***.* Better: *Hours after her triumph, she fell into an* **open manhole***.*

- A meaningless word or phrase only takes up space. Weak writing is full of throwaways like *actually, a bit, kind of, rather, really, somewhat,* and *sort of.* Such fillers are actually sort of habit-forming (see?), so get out of the habit of using them. Wimpy: *Actually, she was* **pretty** *bummed out until she was rescued by a* **really** *hunky sewer worker.* Better: *She was bummed out until she was rescued by a hunky sewer worker.* (There's nothing wrong with using throwaways once in a while to add a bit of informality.)

Catchy is better than blah, online or off. Choose words that are colorful and interesting. But unless you're describing a used car or the trout that got away, hold the hype. In the long run, overselling is as bad as underselling.

8. The Trite Stuff
Nipping Clichés in the Bud

Are the walls of your cubicle closing in? Take a break and drop in on a Web site called Cliché Finder. Just feed in a word, say "love," and out pops a batch of clichés: *love conquers all, puppy love, money can't buy you love, love triangle, love is blind,* and so on.

Most folks, as we all know, don't need a computer to come up with clichés. On the contrary. What they need is one that can replace the tired, overused expressions in their writing with sparkling, original gems that might make the next edition of *Bartlett's*.

Don't hold your breath. Oh, there are programs that can detect triteness in writing. But they miss as much as they find. Our word processor catches *can of worms* and *bite the bullet* but not *beat a dead horse* or *cool as a cucumber*. And it doesn't offer any alternatives, let alone snappy, fresh ones.

Now, a cliché isn't a hanging offense. There are worse things—like two clichés that paint differing pictures: *Cool as a cucumber, Miss Marple decided to bite the bullet.* Or the cliché that sounds silly when taken literally: *In her salad days, Miss Marple enjoyed dressing for dinner.*

When a cliché is right for the occasion and won't make the reader groan, go ahead and use it. We do, as you've probably noticed. In general, though, keep clichés to a minimum. If a tired expression shows up, retire it and rack your brain for something better. Of course, that's easier said than done (groan).

Clichés are tough to avoid because using them is almost a reflex. When you write on automatic pilot, they don't even register on the radar screen (come to think of it, *on automatic pilot* and *on the radar screen* are typical specimens). Phrases become clichés, ironically, because they seem just right—or as a cliché lover would put it, they hit the nail on the head. That's why so many people have used them so often and for so long.

How do you know a cliché when you meet one? Some are obvious. There's a whiff of mothballs about them. Many quaint old clichés (and more than a few newer ones) follow a *blankety-blank* pattern.

There's the *blank as a blank* cliché: *cool as a cucumber, red as a beet, bald as a billiard ball, smart as a whip, cute as a button, busy as a bee, flat as a pancake, crazy as a loon, fresh as a daisy, dead as a doornail, high as a kite, drunk as a skunk, free as a bird, pretty as a picture, fit as a fiddle, proud as a peacock, clear as a bell, white as a sheet, happy as a clam, nutty as a fruitcake, stiff as a board, sharp as a tack, hard as a rock, quiet as a tomb, soft as a baby's bottom,* and *snug as a bug in a rug.*

Then there's the *blanklike blank* cliché: *viselike grip, catlike eyes, deathlike pallor, swanlike neck, snaillike pace, childlike innocence, birdlike appetite,* and *wolflike grin.* And let's not forget the *blankening blank* cliché: *deafening crash, sickening thud, gathering storm, sneaking suspicion, devastating earthquake, finishing touch, raging torrent, withering glance, sweeping change, steaming jungle, grueling ordeal, sleeping giant,* and *burning question.*

An expression doesn't have to be geriatric to be a cliché. If you've heard a trendy phrase a few hundred times in the last year, it's stale. Familiarity, if you'll excuse our saying so, breeds contempt. What once was cutting edge (like *cutting edge*) quickly gets dulled. Use it too many times and your writing gets dull, too.

The Internet age has given birth to a whole generation of clichés in the making—*info highway, multitasking, telecommuting, e-whatever, i-whatever,* and anything with *cyber, com, techno, digital, virtual, wired, dot, Silicon, Web,* or *Net* in it. And that's only a cursory look. These expressions may not be clichés yet (you'll find many in this very book), but keep in touch. For the time being, try not to overuse them. There are enough clichés in the world already.

Platitude Adjustment

If you suspect something is a cliché, it probably is. The list of clichés is endless (no doubt it's a bottomless pit). Some of the usual suspects:

Acid test. Give it an F.

Add insult to injury. A crutch you don't need.

After all is said and done. Enough said.

Agree to disagree. Disagreeable.

An albatross around his neck. Birdbrained.

All walks of life. Get a walker.

Apple of my eye. Seedy.

At first blush. Skin deep.

Back to the drawing board. Sharpen your pencil.

Ball and chain. Heavy-handed (and so is *better half*).

The ball is in your court. Double-fault.

Bated breath (no, not *baited*). A breath of stale air.

Beat a dead horse. Inhumane.

Beat a retreat. Coward.

Behind the eight ball. Dirty pool.

Better late than never. Better never.

Between a rock and a hard place. Ouch.

Bite the bullet. A dud.

Bitter end. R.I.P.

Blessing in disguise. Heaven help us.

Boggles the mind. Yours, maybe.

Bolt from the blue. No electricity.

Bone of contention. Bury it.

Bored to tears. Read a book.

Bosom buddy. Get it off your chest.

Bottom line. Bankrupt.

Broad daylight. Wear shades.

Brute force. A ninety-eight-pound weakling.

By hook or by crook. Off the stage.

Calm before the storm. Waterlogged.

Can of worms. Icky.

Can't see the forest for the trees. Stumped?

Cast a pall. Poor casting.

Champing at the bit (no, not *chomping*). Rein it in.

Checkered career. Forever plaid.

Closure. Get over it.

Count your chickens. Lays an egg.

Crystal clear. Of quartz not.

Cutting edge. Doesn't cut it.

Diamond in the rough. Cubic zirconium.

Draw a blank. So fill it in.

Easier said than done. Then say it.

Fate worse than death. Taxes, maybe?

Fell through the cracks. A dust bunny.

Few and far between. Space invader.

Food for thought. Malnourished.

Fools rush in. Who invited them?

Foregone conclusion. Goes without saying.

Foreseeable future. Ditto.

Garden variety. Needs pruning.

Generation gap. Aging gracelessly.

Get the show on the road. And out of town.

Glass ceiling. Transparent.

Green with envy. Moldy.

Grim reaper. One scythe fits all.

Grind to a halt. Grease it.

Head over heels. Straighten up.

Hear a pin drop. Don't listen.

Hook, line, and sinker. Throw it back.

Hope springs eternal. Hopeless.

Humble abode. What a dump.

Ignorance is bliss. We wouldn't know.

Impenetrable fog. Sound the foghorn.

In no uncertain terms. Terminal.

Innocent bystander. Guilty.

Last but not least. Less than meets the eye.

Leaps and bounds. Skip it.

Leave no stone unturned. Stone cold.

Level playing field. Flat.

Light at the end of the tunnel. Oncoming train?

Like a house afire. Call 911.

Lock, stock, and barrel. Oh, shoot.

Low on the totem pole. Taboo.

Make a killing. DOA.

Mass exodus. Thou shalt not.

Meaningful dialogue. Yackety-yak.

Moment of truth. It's about time.

More than meets the eye. Get glasses.

More the merrier. Not if you're doing the cooking.

Narrow escape. Good riddance.

Needle in a haystack. Lose it.

Never a dull moment. Wanna bet?

Nick of time. Latecomer.

Nip it in the bud. Or wherever.

No sooner said than done. Not soon enough.

One and the same. Pick one.

One fell swoop. One too many.

Pandora's box. Lock securely.

Pay the piper. No tip.

Pet peeve. Fleas?

Place in the sun. Get a parasol.

Play hardball. A strikeout.

Play it by ear. Learn to read music.

Political hopefuls. An also-ran.

Power lunch. Try dieting.

Powers that be. Or not to be.

Preexisting condition. Not covered.

Pushing the envelope. Lick it.

Red-letter day. Needs a vacation.

Reliable source. Why use any other?

Roller coaster. A downer.

Rude awakening. A snooze.

Seat of the pants. Get an alteration.

Shot in the arm. Tetanus, anyone?

Sigh of relief. An old bromide.

Silver lining. A sterling cliché.

Stick out like a sore thumb. Get a Band-Aid.

Stock in trade. Trade it in.

Straw that broke the camel's back. One hump or two?

Take the bull by the horns. After you.

Tarnished image. Think of it as verdigris.

Team player. You're benched.

Thick as thieves. Thin.

Tight ship. Walk the plank.

Till the cows come home. Don't wait up.

Tip of the iceberg. On the rocks.

Tongue in cheek. Even worse, *tongue planted firmly in cheek.*

Torrential rains. A washout.

Tower of strength. Needs steroids.

Trials and tribulations. Think you've got troubles?

Untimely end. Whose isn't?

Viable alternative. Why a bull?

What makes him tick. Off-ticking.

9. Wired Write
Are You Making Sense?

Dan, our agent, is at it again. The manuscripts that cross his desk, he says, are looking better these days but reading worse. The reason? Word processors.

The computer, he's convinced, encourages people to write without thinking. Their words look clean, crisp, and clear on the screen, so naturally the writing must be clean, crisp, and clear, too. Yeah, right.

"I can live with the minor typos, the lost capitals, the idiosyncratic spellings that come with speed, but not the incoherence," Dan says. "For most people, writing well takes time, reflection, and rewriting."

The problem is that most people don't take time to reflect and rewrite. The result is illogical, inconsistent, even silly writing.

The typical e-mailer seldom rereads what he's written before hitting Send or Reply. A second look would tell him that an ill-chosen word or phrase had turned a sensible idea into nonsense: the language might be contradictory or overstated; two words might cancel each other out; a figure of speech might be ridiculous; an expression might read two ways; the numbers might not add up.

Rereading is the best habit you can form. This may be the only time when a postmortem can actually save the patient. We reread every e-mail before sending it, even a short, chatty note to a good friend. And we almost always spot a goof the second time around. Sure, it's usually just a typo. But sometimes it's worse—a lot worse. (Don't ask.) Here are some things to look for when you want to be sure your writing makes sense.

Speaking the Unspeakable

"It's an experience that cannot be described," the first paying tourist in space said on his return to earth. He then proceeded to describe (at length) the indescribable. Well, he had an excuse for sounding spacey. But people with both feet on the ground should choose their words more carefully.

What's wrong here is that many words used loosely for effect have literal meanings, too. Someone may call a Ming vase "priceless," for instance, even though it changed hands for a price only last week at Sotheby's. Or she may call the crème brûlée at the Four Seasons "irresistible" even though she never orders it.

There's nothing wrong with loosely using a word like "priceless" to mean valuable, or "irresistible" to mean tempting, as long as the literal meaning doesn't get in the way. If you call something "priceless," don't put a price on it: *The **priceless** Ming vase sold for $800,000.* If you say something is "irresistible," don't brag about resisting it: *I turned down the **irresistible** crème brûlée.*

When you're using a word for effect, consider any unanticipated special effects:

*The sample sale was an **indescribable** mob scene— crowded, disorganized, and a complete waste of time.* Sounds describable enough.

*In her briefcase the corporate counsel kept legal papers and **unmentionables** like spare panties and bras.* Unless we're mistaken, they were mentioned.

*The **incomparable** Bette Midler has the stage presence of Maria Callas.* Sure looks like a comparison.

*Together we can conquer **insurmountable** obstacles.* And beat the unbeatable foe?

*Mimi found the coffin-shaped canapés **tasteless**.* Were they in poor taste, or were they bland and flavorless?

It's fine to be loose online as long as you don't overlook the literal.

The Superlative Writer

As ex–newspaper editors, we never miss the corrections column in our daily paper. The column would be much shorter, though, if reporters stopped using words like "biggest," "oldest," "richest," "highest," "longest," "coldest," or "fastest" to describe whatever's in the news. More often than not, there's another whatever that's bigger or older or richer or higher or longer or colder or faster.

An alarm bell should go off whenever you use these *est* words or their cousins "first," "most," "worst," and so on (they're called superlatives). If you say somebody was the first to sell a Shakespeare folio on eBay, you'd better be certain. If you don't have time to check, cover your butt. Say that he claimed to be the first or is believed to be the first, but not that he *was* the first.

Some people think a statement without a superlative isn't worth making. A plane crash has to be the *worst* air disaster since whenever. A company's quarterly earnings have to be the *best* in x number of years. A TV flop has to be the *least* popular show in y number of seasons. You can use a superlative in almost any situation. The challenge is using it correctly.

If you're addicted to superlatives, you're probably also hooked on other absolute terms, like "only," "unprecedented," and "unique." An explorer has to be the *only* woman to reach the North Pole by dogsled. The sales of a blockbuster novel have to be *unprecedented*. A new Web browser has to be *unique*. Again, don't use an absolute term unless you're absolutely sure. Just this morning, our local paper had a correction about a first that turned out to be a distant second.

Definite Maybes

Nancy, the former English teacher we've mentioned, used to entertain her ninth-graders with word games. In one, she asked them to think of everyday expressions made up of incompatible words, like "soft rock," "pretty ugly," "good grief," and "alone together."

The term for such a mismatch, "oxymoron," comes from the Greek for "pointedly foolish," which is how people sound when they use one thoughtlessly: *Ally's relationships were **profoundly shallow**. Perry was **intensely relaxed** before the camera. Hannibal was **clearly vague** about his recipe for steak Diane.*

But not all oxymorons sound moronic. Some, like "act naturally," "definite maybe," "taped live," and "working vacation" are accepted idiomatic expressions despite the incongruities. Others, such as "candid pose," "humble pride," "sweet sorrow," and "living dead" (a ninth-grader might add "butt head"), are deliberately ironic or humorous or both.

What makes an oxymoron work? Obviously, the writer has to be in on the joke. If the joke's on him, and the mismatch is inadvertent, he'll sound deeply superficial.

Imagine That

An executive of our acquaintance (we won't name her) recently forwarded us a list of corporate flights of fancy that had landed with a thud in her electronic mailbox. Our favorite? "When the rubber hits the sky." It conjures up the picture of a pickup truck coming to a screeching halt in a cumulus cloud.

We're all for using colorful images to enliven on-line writing, as long as the images make sense. When figures of speech don't figure, however, readers scratch their heads and writers look ridiculous.

Why are there so many wacko images in online writing? The one-word answer is haste. People are in too much of a hurry to see their words through a reader's eyes. The most common mistakes: getting images wrong (*He wears his heart up his sleeve*) and mushing two or more together (*She dug herself into a hole to get the project off the ground*).

The solution is simple. Make a mental picture of each image in your writing. If the image makes sense, go for it. If it's too imaginative (*He paid through the nose for his tissue of lies*), adjust the picture.

Negative Vibes

What do you think of this sentence from an investors' discussion board on the Web? "I'm not biased because I own 200 shares of Intel stock." Are your eyebrows raised? They ought to be.

The sentence could mean two different things: *I'm not biased, even though I own 200 shares of Intel stock.* Or: *I'm biased, but not because I own 200 shares of Intel stock.*

It would have been a simple statement if not for *not*. Why? Well, *because*. A sentence containing both *not* and *because* can be a puzzler. The reader is often left wondering whether *not* refers to what comes before or what comes after *because*. What is and what is *not*?

Take a look at this sentence: *Grete did not go to Boston in April because of the marathon*. It could mean this: *Because of the marathon, Grete did not go to Boston*. Or this: *Grete went to Boston, but not because of the marathon*.

The meaning is uncertain when *not* isn't firmly attached to one thing (the trip to Boston) or another (the marathon). Written without the *not* (*Grete skipped Boston in April because of the marathon*), the sentence becomes clear.

Don't be fooled when *not* is part of a contraction (*isn't, aren't, won't*, and so on): *Grete didn't see the orthopedist because she had shin splints*. It could mean this: *Grete saw the orthopedist, but not because she had shin splints*. Or (though unlikely) this: *Because she had shin splints, Grete didn't see the orthopedist*.

And that's not all. *Not* and *all* can be a puzzling combination, too: *All of the runners don't have sponsors*. The writer probably doesn't mean that none of the runners have sponsors, which is what he's actually saying. Most likely he means: *Not all of the runners have sponsors*. (Or, if we drop the troublesome negative: *Only some of the runners have sponsors*.)

Many writers are also caught flatfooted by *not* statements with numbers in them: *Hundreds did not finish the marathon.* You can bet that millions didn't finish the marathon, including everybody who watched the race at home on TV. Make it: *Hundreds dropped out of the marathon.*

There's always a way to unravel a *not.*

Safety in Numbers

One of our leading news organizations reported recently that Spain earns $10 billion from the meat of the 40,000 bulls killed every year by matadors. Ten *billion?* Really? That comes out to $250,000 for each bull. Come on, now. You don't have to be a cattle rancher to know the real figure must be closer to $250 per bull. Sure enough, we learned later, that $10 billion should have been $10 million.

A lot of the numbers we read, online ones in particular, are bull. People don't take the time to make sure their writing adds up. We're not talking about calculus here. What e-mailers bungle is usually the simple stuff—percentages, proportions, averages, and the number of zeros.

There's no excuse for being numerically challenged these days, since most computers come off the shelf with calculators tucked right into their software. Calculators aside, you can avoid plenty of mistakes just by using your head. If a number seems staggeringly large or incredibly small, maybe it's wrong.

Look again. Common sense can prevent a great many errors.

For starters, you might want to engrave two facts on your brain: The population of the world is somewhat over 6 billion people, and somewhat under 300 million of them live in the United States. In round numbers, that's 6 billion and 300 million. Keep those numbers in mind whenever your writing includes statistics remotely concerned with population, birth or death rates, and consumption or production—worldwide or nationwide or per capita.

Say you're e-mailing a letter to the editor of *Cigar Aficionado* and you want to mention that Americans smoke 600 million cigars a day (you got the figure from your cousin Felipe, who manufactures tobacco wrappers in Miami). Before clicking Send, think for a moment. Six hundred million a day? That would be a couple of cigars for every man, woman, and child in the country. When was the last time you saw a nine-month-old crawling around with a stogie in his mouth? Maybe you should ask your cousin what he's smoking.

Some people worry so much about the trees that they don't see the forest. It's fine to count the trees—that's what calculators are for—but don't forget the forest. If the calculator says you have 1,000 trees but the forest is only a 50-by-100-foot backyard, common sense tells you that something is wrong. Maybe you've punched in a couple of extra zeros. When you think in round numbers and use common sense, you'll make fewer mistakes.

A number of suggestions to help your writing add up:

• Be suspicious of percentages greater than 100. A number that doubles goes up 100 percent, one that triples goes up 200 percent, and so on. When a penny stock climbs to five cents, for example, it increases 400 percent—the four-cent gain. If it's a decrease you're talking about, remember that a number can fall only 100 percent, to zero (unless you're doing negative numbers in math class). No supply of anything—dollars, pretzels, Girl Scouts, cooking sherry, spotted owls—can fall more than 100 percent. Anything over that is a mistake, in this world anyway.

• Don't say something is "*x* times more"—or "*x* times less"—than something else. You're bound to be wrong, or misleading at best. If you say that seventy-six trombones is "two times more" than the original thirty-eight, you're wrong. What you mean is "two times as many." If you say that thirty-eight trombones is "two times less" than seventy-six, you're wrong. What you mean is "half as many."

• Don't add proportions. Average them instead. Let's say a market researcher asks equal numbers of men and women to name their least favorite color. If one of out ten men says chartreuse and three out of ten women say chartreuse, what proportion of respondents say chartreuse? The answer is two in ten (the average of one and three), not four in ten (the sum of one and three). And by the way, never mix proportions unless there are equal numbers in each group. If you do, you're averaging apples and orangutans.

• Be careful with increases and decreases. Say the local library's bookmobile budget is going up, but not as much as it did last year. That doesn't mean the budget is decreasing, only that the increase is smaller. Or say the bookmobile's operating hours have been cut back this year, but not as much as in neighboring towns. That doesn't mean the hours have increased, just that the decrease is less than it might have been.

• Don't confuse *average, median,* and *mean.* These aren't interchangeable, so you shouldn't toss them around casually. Suppose you have three computers at home—one, two, and nine years old. The *average* age is four: that's the sum of the ages (twelve) divided by the number of computers (three). The *median* age is two: the number that's in the middle when the three ages are arranged by size. (If there were an even number of ages, you'd have to add the middle pair and divide by two.) The *mean,* also called the *arithmetic mean,* is four, the same as the *average.* (Some dictionaries define *mean* more loosely as the midpoint between two extremes, which in this case would be five.)

There will be no pop quiz tomorrow, class.

10. Get a Virtual Life
Operating Instructions

David Owens, an academic type who studies the world of real-life Dilberts, examined thousands of e-mail messages exchanged by employees at a technology company over several years. His findings should be of interest to anyone toiling away in the cubicles of corporate America.

Low-level employees, he found, used a lot of smileys, catchy graphics, abbreviations, jokes, and heartwarming quotes in their e-mail. Mid-level managers wrote long, dyspeptic e-mails with loads of jargon, then copied them to half the office. The big shots sent curt, poorly written messages with rotten spelling and grammar.

You might conclude from this study that the best way to make it up the corporate ladder is to write crummy e-mail. Before you uninstall your spell-checker, though, you should know that the company in the Owens study is now defunct.

Would better e-mail have saved that business? Perhaps not, though you never know. Technology hasn't changed the fact that good writing helps you communicate better. And anything that helps you communicate better is great, whether you're a trainee just out of college, an ambitious middle manager, or a grizzled boss trying to goose the bottom line.

It would be nice if the computer on your desk or in your lap could do the communicating for you. But a word processor can only process words. You have to do the writing yourself.

How do you know if your writing clicks? Ask yourself these twenty questions before hitting Send. You don't have to answer all of them every time you e-mail an old roommate or a close colleague who may be able to read your mind. Try to answer as many as you can, however, especially when the message really matters.

1. **Is the subject line helpful?** The reader should be able to tell at a glance what you're writing about and how urgent it is. She's as busy as you are, and she needs to know which messages to handle first. Imagine her overflowing in-basket and have mercy. (See chapters 1 and 2.)

2. **Did you get right to the point?** Computer users have short attention spans. Don't expect them to scroll through more than a screenful to find out what's up. You don't have to be rude or abrupt, but

state your business somewhere in the first few sentences. (See chapter 6.)

3. **Is the language clear?** Don't obscure your message with techie talk, trendy terms, humongous words, and convoluted sentences. That doesn't mean you have to dumb down your writing or be boring and trite. Impress the reader with your ideas, not with your vocabulary. (See chapters 4, 7, and 9.)

4. **Did you say too much?** Try not to write more than you have to, certainly at work. Long e-mails are read last. If you're passing along an article or a report or something else from a third party, don't copy or forward the whole thing (complete with routing gibberish). Cut and paste only the relevant parts. (See chapters 2 and 6.)

5. **Are your facts right?** Be *really* sure of your information, not just *virtually* sure. It's all right to be informal, but not with facts. And check the math (a slide in earnings, remember, is not necessarily a loss). As for the Internet, it's full of misinformation, so be careful about what you pass on. (See chapters 5 and 9.)

6. **Did you say what you're replying to?** When you click Reply, a cryptic "Fine" or "Nope" or "Maybe later" won't do. Never make the reader guess which message you're answering, definitely not if time has passed. You're not the only person he's e-mailed. Don't repeat his original message in its entirety,

though. If a brief mention isn't enough, cut and paste only what he needs to know. (See chapters 1, 2, and 6.)

7. **Were you polite?** Small slights are magnified in e-mail and other online writing, and offhand remarks can be taken the wrong way. Show some sensitivity. Ask for something, don't demand it. Familiarize yourself with "please," "thank you," and "sorry." And don't request an immediate reply, particularly if your message is long or complicated or unsolicited. (See chapters 1 and 4.)

8. **Were you discreet?** Assume that anything you send can and will be used against you. No, it's not paranoia. Office e-mail isn't the place for sensitive personnel matters, criticism of third parties, off-color remarks, romance, gossip, rumors, or tooting your own horn. Protect other people's privacy at home and at work. Don't share someone's e-mail address without permission, even inadvertently. When you send multiple messages, use blind copies so each person sees only his own address. (See chapters 1, 2, and 3.)

9. **Did you add a greeting and a closing?** Take the chill out of e-mail. Begin and end your message on a personal note. There's nothing analog about being friendly. The seconds spent adding a "Hi, Tom" and a "Bye, Sally" could change the course of human events. (See chapter 2.)

10. **Is the attachment welcome?** Before you attach that spreadsheet or home video or musical interlude to your e-mail, think about the reader. Are you sure she wants it and has the software to make sense of it? (See chapters 2 and 6.)

11. **Did you use the shift key?** Capitalize properly. Use both big and small letters—not all one or the other. E-mail that's all upper- or lowercase is hard to read, and e-mail that's all caps is considered rude. Don't be a shiftless writer. (See chapter 1.)

12. **Did you break for paragraphs?** Please, no solid blobs of type. Break your message into bite-sized pieces, one short paragraph per subject. It'll be easier to read and easier to answer. Magically, you'll look more organized, too. (See chapters 1 and 7.)

13. **Will the reader get the shorthand?** Not everybody understands the smileys, abbreviations, and insider jargon that worm their way into e-mail. If you and your reader share the same slanguage, go ahead and use it. Otherwise, stick to plain English. (See chapters 4 and 7.)

14. **Will the joke fall flat?** Those strings of jokes that clog so many in-baskets aren't universally appreciated. Be selective about what you send and to whom. If you copy six screenfuls of lightbulb jokes to everybody in your address book, you're bound to offend someone. (See chapter 3.)

15. **Does this look like spam?** Nothing's wrong with talking up a pet project, but there's a thin line be-

tween legitimate promotion and spam. Keep hype out of the subject line, and personalize each message. If something reads like indiscriminate bulk mail, it probably is. (See chapter 3.)

16. **Do all these people need copies?** Fight litter on the information highway. You don't have to copy your every idea to everyone in your seminar or sales group or alumni association or address book. Everybody else's mailbox is just as stuffed as yours. (See chapters 2 and 3.)

17. **Should you sleep on it?** Never e-mail in the heat of anger. You'll regret it the next day. If there's steam shooting out your ears, cool off—and cool your message off—before you click Send. (See chapters 1 and 3.)

18. **Does it have to be an e-mail?** E-mail is swell, but it's not always appropriate. Maybe a letter or a phone call or a face-to-face meeting would be better. Don't e-mail the guy in the next cubicle, for instance, when it would be more efficient to get up and walk a few feet. (See chapter 3.)

19. **Did you read it again?** Everybody finds mistakes the second time around. Just imagine the time you'll save on damage control the next day. Think of rereading as time saved, not time wasted. (See chapter 9.)

20. **Did you check the grammar, spelling, and punctuation?** Keep a dictionary and a grammar guide on your desk, and don't use them as paperweights.

Be sure every word means what you think it means. Spell-checkers? They aren't perfect, but make a habit of using yours—with a skeptical eye. Grammar-checkers, in our opinion, are a waste of time. (See chapters 11, 12, 13, and 14.)

Oh, come now! Why the long face? Surely you didn't expect to sail through the book without having to deal with grammar, usage, spelling, and punctuation? These things don't take care of themselves. And you can't ignore them online, no matter what anyone says. Read on. We'll try to make it as painless as possible.

PART III

Words of Passage

11. Grammar à la Modem
A Crash Course

We were looking for an excuse to quit working one day, so we called up Google, our search engine of choice at the time, and typed in some things we had on our minds (it was almost lunchtime). Care to see the results?

Apple pie	203,000 hits
Burgers	280,000 hits
Fries	351,000 hits
Hot dogs	454,000 hits
Grammar	812,000 hits

Yes, that's right. Netheads are four times as likely to have grammar on the brain as apple pie, according to our unscientific Web survey. (And that's not counting tens of thousands of hits from people who spell it "grammer.")

If you're one of those who believe language doesn't matter online, look around. The Web is teeming with grammar guides and grammar quizzes, grammar clubs and grammar hotlines. Discussion groups and the like are patrolled by grammar cops waiting to nab anybody who confuses *their* and *there* or *its* and *it's*. As for e-mail, who hasn't heard a horror story that would make Strunk and White turn in their graves?

Apparently, good English *is* a big deal, and sometimes even a deal breaker. Take *your* and *you're*, for example. Let's say a decorator and her well-heeled client plan to discuss his new beach house over lunch. She finds out he's sprained an ankle on the polo field and sends him this e-mail: "I just heard you're bad news. Forget about lunch." She meant well, but because of her unfortunate use of *you're* instead of *your*, she may have to forget the commission, too.

Okay, readers can usually figure out what you mean. But you'll get no respect if they have to do your work for you. That fantastic idea of yours might be ridiculed or even dismissed, all because of a silly lapse in grammar.

Most people will cut you some slack when you write online. They don't use perfect, formal English in their e-mails and they won't demand it of yours. There's a difference, though, between relaxing your standards and dumping them in the Recycle Bin. If you want your writing taken seriously, take seriously what you write. All things considered, we'd rather sound a little stuffy than a little stupid.

Online writers have found virtually endless ways to butcher their grammar. We won't get into every one here, but we'll try to help you avoid some of the

most common—and embarrassing—blunders seen
in cyberspace.

The I Generation

Avi, a journalist who lives in suburban Washington, D.C., was flabbergasted one day when his
second-grade daughter "corrected" his English at the
dinner table. He'd used the phrase "for Mommy and
me," and she protested that he should have said "for
Mommy and *I*." Teacher says so, she insisted; it has
to be *I*, not *me*.

Since Avi edits and writes for a living, this inci-
dent made his hair stand on end. He knew very well
that *me* is correct, so he did some checking. And yes,
the teacher was telling her students to use *I* and *me*
the wrong way. She had them change *me* to *I* in perfectly correct sentences like *It's a secret between you
and me* and *Mom scolded Jenny and me.*

Mistakenly using *I* for *me* is probably the most
common grammatical error in English, online as well
as off. Nobody (no grown-up, anyway) messes up
when *I* or *me* is used alone. No one says *Don't cry for
I* or *Meet I in St. Louis.* Yet people mess up all the
time when *I* or *me* is part of a pair. They say things
like *Don't cry for **Juan and I*** or *Meet **Judy and I** in St.
Louis.*

Why are people driven to use *I* instead of *me* in a
pair? Maybe it has something to do with the way
we're brought up. (Hey, let's blame our parents!) As

kids, we learn *me* before *I,* and we use it a lot—often incorrectly: "*Me* want Potato Head!" And because we're constantly corrected ("No, dear, *I* want Potato Head"), we get the impression that *I* is a better, classier word than *me.*

No wonder so many people think *I* is always right in a twosome. And so many others pick *I* over *me* when they're not sure which is right. (Some mistakenly opt for *myself*—a problem we'll get to next.)

Here's the deal with *I* and *me.* Whatever is right by itself will be right in a pair, so mentally eliminate the other guy: *Don't cry for [Juan and]* **me.** *Meet [Judy and]* **me** *in St. Louis.*

Song of Myself

If online writing is any indication, people are growing more *self*-centered every day. Have you noticed? They can't keep themselves out of their writing.

"This will be worked out between the art director and *myself,*" an editor e-mails. Shame on her! Any self-respecting editor would have written "between the art director and *me.*"

People who are unsure whether to use *I* or *me* often use *myself* instead. That's cheating. (For help with *I* and *me,* see the previous section.) The *self* words—*himself, herself, itself, ourselves, themselves,* and the rest—weren't created to give us an easy way out.

Never use a *self* word in place of an ordinary pronoun (*I, me, he, him, she, her*, and so on). Use it only for emphasis (*I heard it **myself***) or to refer to someone or something already mentioned (*The art director threatened to throw **himself** out the window*).

The It Squad

When we read our e-mail, we're always amazed at how many otherwise literate types are done in by the *it* squad. Everyone knows how to use *it*, but add an *s*—or should that be *'s*?—to the end, and quite a few smart people reach their wits' end. They can't tell their *its* from their *it's*. Luckily, this one is a no-brainer. If every grammar glitch were so easy to fix, we'd all sound like Bill Buckley.

Its (no apostrophe, please) is a possessive, a word showing ownership, like *his* or *her* or *Harry's*. But *it's* is a contraction, two words (*it is* or *it has*) mushed into one, with an apostrophe standing for whatever is missing.

There's an easy way to get with *its* and *it's*. When you could use *it is* or *it has* and still make sense, *it's* is right. Otherwise, choose *its*. *My pit bull's bark is scary, but **it's** not as scary as **its** bite.*

If you want to blame somebody for the confusion here, blame Harry. Since words like *Harry's* are possessives, many well-meaning people assume *it's* must be, too. They assume too much.

Help for the Whomless

When we were growing up, Pat in the Midwest and Stewart on the East Coast, our English teachers made sure everyone knew the difference between *who* and *whom*. What's the story now? Do we still need both of them? Or did *whom* pass away with the twentieth century?

Many people seem to think *whom* is ancient history, if they think of it at all. But *whom* isn't quite ready to give up the ghost. Yes, we hear a death rattle every now and then, and *who* can't wait to inherit *whom*'s estate. Yet just when we think *whom* is resting in peace, the corpse sits up and shouts, "Aha!"

You can get away with dropping *whom* in much of your online writing (in chat rooms or instant messages or e-mails with like-minded folks). But you'll get nailed on public bulletin boards, mailing lists, and such. And work is no place for the *whom*less, unless you're El Supremo and don't care what the rank and file think.

See if you can solve this whodunit: *Lucy couldn't remember [**who** or **whom**] gave the Vitameatavegamin to [**who** or **whom**].*

If you're not sure, ask yourself this question: *Who is doing what to **whom**?* Now, let's try again: *Lucy couldn't remember **who** gave the Vitameatavegamin to **whom**.*

That wasn't so bad. Things grow confusing, however, when extra words come between *who* and what

it's doing, or between *whom* and what's being done to
it: *So [**who** or **whom**], Lucy wondered for the umpteenth
time, gave the Vitameatavegamin to heaven knows [**who**
or **whom**]?*

If you're stuck, mentally strip away the surplus: *So
who ... gave the Vitameatavegamin **to** ... **whom**?*

Sometimes, *to* not only gets separated from *whom*
but also ends up after it: *Ethel couldn't remember **whom**
she gave the Vitameatavegamin **to**.* If you move the key
words around in your mind and bring them back together (*... **to whom** she gave the Vitameatavegamin*), it
becomes clear *who* did what to *whom*.

Once more, the important thing to remember is
that *who* does something and something is done to
(or *at, by, for, in, on, upon, with*) *whom*.

Disagreeable Matters

Peter, a friend of many talents, does a great imi-
tation of Henry Kissinger singing "Luck, Be a Lady."
Imagine a stuffy German-accented diplomat portray-
ing the slick gambler in *Guys and Dolls*.

Not to be too theatrical, there's a point to be
made here. If you're not trying to be funny when
you write online, be sure the actors in your sentences
(that is, the subjects) are right for their roles (the verbs).

Usually it's no big deal to match the actor and the
action—to make subject and verb agree. By and large
the choice is automatic. A singular subject (*Rosencrantz*)
gets a singular verb (*is*): *Rosencrantz **is** dead.* A plural

subject (*Rosencrantz and Guildenstern*) gets a plural verb (*are*): Rosencrantz and Guildenstern **are** dead.

But sometimes it's harder to figure out whether a subject is singular or plural, and the right verb isn't so obvious. Which of these would you choose?

*Rosencrantz, together with his pal Guildenstern, [**is** or **are**] dead.*
*A number of the Elsinore gang [**is** or **are**] under suspicion.*
*None of their alibis [**make** or **makes**] sense.*
*Either the capons or the ale [**was** or **were**] poisoned.*

You were right if you deduced that Rosencrantz, together with his pal Guildenstern, *is* dead, that a number of the Elsinore gang *are* under suspicion, that none of their alibis *make* sense (no, *none* isn't always singular, as you'll see), and that either the capons or the ale *was* poisoned. If you got them wrong, these simple rules may help next time:

- Extra padding between the subject and the verb won't change the verb. Don't be fooled by phrases like *together with, in addition to, along with,* and *as well as.* Rosencrantz is one guy, and he's still one guy even when other things are mentioned in passing: *Rosencrantz, along with the entire population of Elsinore and despite the efforts of three physicians using leeches and poultices, **is** dead.*

- Words like *number, total,* and *majority* can be either plural or singular, depending on what you mean. Are you talking about many things, or one? If you mean the individuals in the group, use a plural verb: *A number of gang members **are** suspects*. If you mean the group as a whole, use a singular: *The number **is** staggering*. Clue: Look at the word in front—is it *a* or *the*? Usually *a number, a total*, and *a majority* (especially when followed by *of*) will be plural. But *the number, the total*, and *the majority* will generally be singular.

- Words like *none, any*, and *all* can be either singular or plural, depending on whether you're talking about an *it* or a *them*. Mentally inserting the words *of it* or *of them* can help you choose the right verb: *Eight alibis, and none [of them] **make** sense. A long-winded alibi, and none [of it] **makes** sense.* (If you've been taught that *none* is always singular, you've been misinformed. See the grammar myths at the end of this chapter.)

- In *either...or* and *neither...nor* sentences, the subject comes in two parts. What do you do if one part is singular and the other plural? Couldn't be easier. Take your cue from the part that's closer to the verb: *Either the ale or the capons **were** poisoned. Neither the capons nor the ale **was** tested.*

Why bother with all this? Because an agreeable sentence is a readable one.

Cultured Plurals

Most of the time, a single thing multiplies with very little fuss—in writing, if not in biology. With the simple addition of *s,* a *rabbit* turns into *rabbits,* *fear* grows into *fears, revelation* leads to *revelations, doubt* swells to *doubts,* and *hope* begets *hopes.*

Some words don't multiply so simply, though. Instead of *s,* you might have to add *es* or *ies* or do something completely different to make a singular word plural. The choice isn't always clear. One rendezvous is a rendezvous, but what are two? And how do you keep up with more than one Jones? These are the preferred solutions to the more difficult multiplication problems.

- Words ending in *y*: If the *y* comes after a vowel (*a, e, i, o, u*), add only *s. Wild **turkeys** avoid **guys** with loaded **toys** before the **holidays.*** If the *y* comes after a consonant (a letter like *b, d, l, m, r, t*), drop the *y* and add *ies. **Ladies** with big **salaries** don't bring yellow **stickies** and backup **floppies** to office **parties.***

- Words ending in *o*: Most add just an *s. **Flamingos** and **hippos** have no patience with **bozos** and **bimbos.*** There are very few exceptions, most of them in this example: *The **heroes** arrived as the **tornadoes** were tossing **cargoes** of **potatoes** and **tomatoes** around like **mosquitoes.***

- Words ending in *ch, s, sh, x,* or *z*: Add *es. Sigmund dreamed of **foxes** wearing **galoshes** and **witches** sipping gin **fizzes.***

- Names: Add *s* in most cases, but add *es* if the name ends in *ch, s, sh, x,* or *z.* (Don't change *y* to *ies* in names.) *There are three **Beths,** two **Rachels,** and two*

*Felixes in the acupuncture class, but no **Harrys** and no **Joneses.***

- Unchanging words: Some words, most of them from the animal world and a few others ending in *s*, don't change. *Many **elk** and **moose** behaved like **swine** at their spring and fall **rendezvous**, according to wildlife officials at the two **headquarters** monitoring them.*

- You choose: Some words become plural in two different ways. *You say **scarfs** and I say **scarves**, you say **wharfs** and I say **wharves**—let's call the whole thing off.*

- Numbers and letters: Opinions differ, but we recommend adding an apostrophe to separate the *s* from the number or letter. *While **a's** and **i's** are vowels, **6's** and **7's** are digits.* But no apostrophe with spelled-out numbers: *The experts were at **sixes** and **sevens**.*

- Oddities: What can we say, except that English has its phenomena? *Geese, **mice**, **oxen**, and **bacteria** all produce **children**, given the right **criteria**.*

What Possessed You?

If there's one thing you ought to get right when you write, it's who owns what. Possession, after all, is nine points of the law. In writing, the point to consider is the apostrophe, the punctuation mark between the *g* and the *s* in Kellogg's Rice Krispies.

Look what a difference an apostrophe can make.

*The cheapskate client is **Mr. Buttons*** means the client is named Mr. Buttons. *The cheapskate client is **Mr. Button's*** means the cheapskate is one of Mr. Button's clients.

The location of the apostrophe makes a big difference, too. *The fishy balance sheet was the **auditor's** fault* means only one poor slob is to blame. *The fishy balance sheet was the **auditors'** fault* means the guilty party has company.

Here's the scoop on using apostrophes to protect your possessions:

- Add *'s* to singular words, including names, regardless of their endings: ***Mavis's** husband, **Alice's** boyfriend, and **Ms. Molyneux's** brother got into a drunken row at **FedEx's** Christmas party, according to **Liz's** e-mail.*
- Add *'s* to plurals that don't already end in *s*: *As the **men's** voices got louder, the **women's** patience ran out.*
- Add only an apostrophe to plurals ending in *s*: *When the men started throwing **frogs'** legs at the **executives'** table, the women hustled them into the **Joneses'** van with the help of the **Browns'** daughter.*

Got the point?

Tense and Tense-ability

When our generation learned how to tell time, we had to figure out what it meant if the big hand was on the six and the little hand was on the three. Today all a child has to do is glance at his digital watch or her computer monitor. But one thing about time hasn't changed. You still can't go back to the future, unless you're watching Marty McFly on your VCR.

Words are another matter. It's easy to time-travel in your online writing, as long as you don't lose your tenses—past, present, future, and so on. A sentence that begins in the past or present and travels to the future will end up in a time warp if the tenses don't work together.

Try your hand at these: *Doc Brown told Marty last week that he [will or would] get the plutonium fuel on Friday. Now Doc tells him he [will or would] get it on Sunday.*

Here's a clue. Check out the tense of the first verb. If it's in the past (like *told*), use *would*; if it's in the present (like *tells*), use *will. Doc Brown told Marty last week that he would get the plutonium fuel on Friday. Now Doc tells him he will get it on Sunday.*

The same thing works for *may* and *might*. If the first verb is in the present, use *may*. If it's in the past, use *might. Doc Brown told Marty last week that he might get the plutonium fuel on Friday. Now Doc tells him he may get it on Sunday.*

See? Nothing to get tense about.

Laying It On

Words don't have to be long to be confusing. Ask everyone who's ever mixed up *lie* and *lay*—and that means a good part of the English-speaking population.

Even those who use *lie* and *lay* correctly in the present tense may screw them up in the past. That's understandable, because the various forms look and sound so alike. The past tense of one is spelled like the present of the other.

To unscramble *lie* and *lay*, remember that to *lie* is to *recline*, while to *lay* is to *place* (they almost rhyme, don't they?). This is how the various tenses work.

*As a rule, Dilbert's laptop **lies** on his desk. Yesterday it **lay** there. For weeks it **has lain** there.*

*Usually Dilbert **lays** the laptop on his desk. Yesterday he **laid** it there. For weeks he **has laid** it there.*

Commit them to memory, then go lie down. (And by the way, the word that means *fib* is a different word entirely. Would we lie to you?)

Over There

Computer users are remarkably casual about *their* writing. Or is it *there* writing? Or *they're* writing? (Hint: Forget you ever saw the last two sentences.)

For writers of all kinds, *their, there,* and *they're* cause more than their share of trouble. But they shouldn't, since each one has the clue to its identity built right in. Let's look at the clues.

Their is a possessive, and conveniently it contains the word *heir.* Who's more concerned with ownership than an heir? ***Their laptops are missing.***

There refers to a place, like *here*. Luckily, the word *here* is right there. *The computers aren't there.*

They're, a contraction, is short for *they are.* Appropriately, *they* is therein. *They're gone.*

A little rhyme may help:

If their laptops aren't there,
Then they're in for repair.

You're the Top

Stewart got spammed the other day. The subject line of the e-mail (deleted unread, of course) proclaimed "YOUR IN LUCK!!!" Aside from the overabundance of caps and exclamation points, the spammer had a problem with his grammar. The word he wanted was *you're.*

Spammers aren't the only ones who mix up *your* and *you're.* If we ignored every e-mail that had them wrong, we'd miss a lot of important news.

It's not hard to tell them apart. *Your* is used for only one thing—to show possession. *You're,* short for *you are,* is a contraction. *Take your spread sheets and go! You're fired!*

Iffy Lube

At one time or another, most of us dream of having money to burn. Remember Tevye singing "If I Were a Rich Man"? But why did he use *were* instead of *was*?

Something weird happens to English when we're in an iffy frame of mind (grammarians call this mood the subjunctive). The word *was* in a statement like *I **was** a rich man* often becomes *were* when *if* is added: *If I **were** a rich man.*

We use this iffy kind of writing when a sentence or a clause (a group of words with a subject and its verb) begins with *if* and isn't true: *If Tevye **were** a rich man, he'd build a big, tall house with rooms by the dozen.* Tevye isn't a rich man, so *was* becomes *were.*

But when an *if* statement is—or even could be—true, *was* doesn't change. *If Tevye **was** the father of five daughters, he must have learned a lot about women.* Tevye is the father of five daughters, so *was* remains *was.* Or: *If Tevye's wife **was** mean to him, she should apologize.* Tevye's wife may indeed have been mean to him, so *was* is still *was.*

We also use this iffy way of writing when we're in a wishful frame of mind, even when there's no *if* in sight: *Tevye wishes he **were** a rich man.* Or: *Tevye wishes his oldest daughter **were** in love with the butcher, not the tailor.*

Who's Afraid of Whose?

In conversations around the water cooler, it makes no difference whether you say *who's* or *whose.* They're both pronounced "hooze," so who's to know? Too bad you can't get off that easy at the keyboard. One thing we've learned in the age of e-mail is that there's nothing like writing to reveal the gaps in our grammar. Mixing up *who's* and *whose* is a dead give-away, as in this embarrassing example: ***Who's** idea was it to put pink paper in the copier, and **whose** going to change the tray?* (Reverse the two and you have it right.) This is how to sort them out.

Who's is short for *who is* or *who has.* The clue is the apostrophe, which stands for the missing letters. ***Who's** angling for the job Myra used to have?*

Whose is the possessive. It shows who possesses something. ***Whose** job is Myra angling for?*

Suggestion: If you can substitute *who is* or *who has,* go for *who's.*

Which Craft

From the looks of the typical e-mail, you'd think the words *which* and *that* were as interchangeable as background colors on a desktop. Not so. And getting them wrong is a sign of sloppy writing.

We may be losing the distinction between these words, but it's not lost yet. Here's the story on whether a clause (a group of words with a subject and a verb) should begin with *that* or *which.*

- If you can drop the clause and the main point of the sentence stays the same, use *which*: *The software upgrade, **which sells at Staples for $199,** can be downloaded free.* (With or without the *which* clause, the main point is that the software can be down-loaded free.)

• If you drop the clause and the main point of the sentence is lost, use *that*: *A software upgrade **that can be downloaded free** sells at Staples for $199.* (Without the *that* clause, the main point is lost.)

Tip: A *which* clause generally goes inside commas; a *that* clause doesn't. A memory aid might help:

> *Commas, **which** show what to pare,*
> *Aren't used when **that** is there.*

As You Like It

In a more innocent time, the slogan "Winston tastes good like a cigarette should" upset English teachers more than it did doctors. These days, the big cigarette companies are on the defensive, and so is the word *as.* Have the rules for using *like* and *as* changed?

No, *Winston tastes good **as** a cigarette should* is still correct. *As,* not *like,* should be used when it's followed by a clause, a group of words with both a subject and a verb. If there's no verb, use *like*: *Despite its filter, Winston tastes **like** a cigarette.*

But the grounds are shifting. In casual writing, which includes much of what you see online, *like* is gaining on *as.* We're not ready to throw in the towel, though. The informal use of *like* to introduce a clause may be all right in a chat room or an instant message or an e-mail to a friend, but not when it's important to be grammatically correct, perhaps on a company Web page or in a memo to the chairman of the board.

If you want to be right, think of the old Winston commercial—and do otherwise.

Checkmate

In the wrong hands, a fully loaded grammar-checker can be a dangerous thing. In the right hands, it can be a lot of laughs. In any hands, it isn't very good at what it's supposed to be doing—checking grammar.

The day may come when some whiz kid invents a grammar-checker that does more good than harm, but don't hold your breath. Even the best of the lot are, to put it charitably, inadequate and misinformed. They can lead to writing that's stilted, awkward, confusing, and—worst of all—full of grammatical errors.

But for cheap amusement, it's hard to beat a grammar-checker. Try one sometime. Run a perfectly decent piece of writing—say, an op-ed piece or a humor column—through the checker. Then take cover as the ridiculous suggestions, blatant misconceptions, and wacky sentence constructions come flying at you.

Just for fun, we put a three-page article by Bill Gates through the grammar-checker in his Microsoft Word program. Wouldn't you know it? The software found dozens of problems in his article, including writing that was too wordy, passive, unpersuasive, personal, informal, and fragmented.

We're not suggesting that Bill go back to Harvard and finish his education. Actually, he did a pretty good job, and we disagreed with every single nitpick (including the one about "pretty good job"). Maybe he should send his programmers back to grammar school.

The subject of his article? It was spam, which, by the way, the software said he should have spelled with a capital *S*.

Body Politics

In physics, a body at rest tends to remain at rest and a body in motion tends to remain in motion. In grammar, a *body* word, whether moving or not, remains singular—unless somebody slips up. And somebody always does. There's something about *body* words (*anybody, everybody, nobody, somebody*, and their cousins *anyone, everyone*, and so on) that drives us to make them plural. Even people who know better often do it automatically.

Nobody blows a simple sentence like this: *Everyone always bonds at the corporate retreat.* Or this: *Is anybody venting about Systems Support?*

The trouble comes when you have to refer to that *everyone* or *anybody* later: *Everyone bonds when* **they** *share experiences*, or *If anybody vents, calm* **them** *down.* Uh-oh. A singular *everyone* has magically become a plural *they,* and a singular *anybody* is now a plural *them.* That's cheating.

Nobody, not even Harry Potter, really believes *anybody* can be singular one moment and plural the next. So why do people use *they, them,* and *their* to refer to *everybody* and company?

Maybe they don't want to write *Everyone bonds when **he** shares experiences,* or *If anybody vents, calm **him or her** down.* Those examples are correct, but some would consider one sexist and the other clunky.

Enter *they* and *them.* Apparently it's better to cheat than to sound awkward or politically incorrect. Or is it?

Now, most people don't think about politics or style when they write. The words *they* and *them* simply pop into their minds. And as more and more folks use plurals that way, the choice becomes instinctive. That's how English changes.

Change may indeed be coming, but it ain't here yet. It's still bad grammar to use *they, them,* and *their* with *body* language. When your English has to be at its best, especially on the job, keep *everybody* and *anybody* (and all the words that refer to them) singular.

If you don't want to sound sexist or awkward, reword your writing. Instead of *Everyone bonds when **he** shares experiences,* try *Everyone bonds when sharing experiences.* Instead of *If anybody vents, calm **him or her** down,* try *Calm down anyone who vents.*

There's always a way.

Myth Information

Some time back, newspapers on both sides of the Atlantic were abuzz when a couple of new dictionaries pointed out that it's all right to split infinitives. (It was a slow news week.) The journalists seemed unaware that it's always been correct to split infinitives, and dictionaries have been saying so for ages. The so-called rule against splitting infinitives is one of several myths about English that refuse to die, despite the best efforts of grammarians to dispose of them. Let's discard some of the more notorious ones.

🗑 Don't use contractions (words like *can't, she's,* and *we're*). Wrong! The contraction, two words combined into one, is entirely acceptable English and has been for centuries.

🗑 Don't use prepositions (*by, for, of, with,* and so on) at the end of sentences. Not so fast! The preposition, a positioning word, has been used at the end of sentences from the early days of English, despite the efforts of some eighteenth- and nineteenth-century classicists to make the language more like Latin.

🗑 Don't start a sentence with a conjunction (such as *and* or *but*). Why not? The conjunction, a connecting word, can be used to join words, phrases, clauses, and (yes) sentences.

🗑 Don't use *none* as a plural. Not true! In fact, *none* can be either singular or plural, depending on whether you mean *none of it* or *none of them*. (***None** of the money **was** allocated because **none** of the purchases **were** approved*.)

🗑 Don't ever use double negatives. Wrong again! Not every double negative is a no-no. Some can come in handy: *in no uncertain terms* or *it's not impossible* or *she's not untrustworthy.*

🗑 Don't split infinitives. Says who? There's nothing wrong with putting something between the *to* and the infinitive in a phrase like *to see* (for example, *to clearly see the difference*), as long as the writing isn't awkward. The old belief is a misconception, a misguided attempt to apply Latin grammar to English. Grammarians have been trying to debunk it for generations.

12. Go Configure
Abused, Confused,
and Misused Words

We exchanged e-mails some years ago with a twenty-something executive from Silicon Valley. We'd sent him a suggestion and he messaged us back, "I'll run some cycles on that." We had no idea what he meant, but we didn't want to be so uncool as to ask him. Instead, we found a computer-literate friend who was able to translate for us.

"I'll run some cycles on that" was cyberspeak for "I'll think about it," according to Simon, a literary agent in Manhattan. We thanked him and said we'd file the expression in our gray cells for future reference. "Don't bother," he said. "It's just a flavor-of-the-week phrase. It won't mean the same thing next week." Simon was right. We haven't seen it since, though other versions of the "cycle" idea keep cropping up like variations on a theme.

Instant expressions come and go at warp speed these days. Quite a few folks, not just technoweenies, like to sprinkle their online writing with trendy jargon to show the rest of humanity how up-to-the minute they are. Surprising us with a word we don't know—something with the life span of a fruit fly—is their way of saying "Gotcha!" Well, let them have their little game. It doesn't matter a whole lot in the grand scheme of things.

What does matter is that many fine words are being lost because of neglect and abuse. Some have been mauled so badly, especially in online writing, that they're on life support. Others may be breathing without assistance, but their conditions range from fair to critical.

Why should we care? Because these words are everything words should be—clear, precise, efficient, and above all, useful. With neglect, they become fuzzy, imprecise, feeble, and ultimately useless. Thankfully, it's not too late to revive them. Let's take a look at the most common words on the wounded list.

affect/effect. If you want an action word (a verb), *affect* is probably right. *The ergonomic chair didn't affect Wally's lower-back pain.* If you want a word for a thing (a noun), *effect* is a good bet. *The new keyboard had no effect on Tina's carpal tunnel syndrome.* Less commonly, *affect* is used as a noun meaning "feeling," and *effect* as a verb meaning "to bring about." *Phil's lack of affect made him unable to effect change.*

aggravate/irritate. If you *irritate* something, you inflame it; if you *aggravate* something, you make it worse. *Mammy Yokum irritated Pappy's tender skin every time she gave him a bath, and she aggravated the situation by using a scrub brush.* Oh, and don't use *aggravate* to mean "bother" or "annoy." That's irritating.

among/between. Use *between* when referring to two things, *among* for three or more. *Dino hid between Pebbles and Bamm Bamm while Fred mingled among the guests.*

bad/badly. *Bad,* an adjective, describes a thing or condition, and *badly,* an adverb, describes an action. *Linus felt bad whenever he played badly.* Anyone who feels *badly,* by the way, has a lousy sense of touch.

bring/take. The choice depends on your point of view. If your mind is on the start of the trip, use *take.* If it's on the end, *bring* is the thing. *Nancy takes jelly doughnuts from the cafeteria and brings them to Sluggo.* Keep your eye on the goodies as they come and go. If they're coming, use *bring*; if they're going, use *take.*

can/may. No, they're not the same. When you *can* do something, you're able to do it; when you *may* do something, you're permitted to do it. *Alley Oop says Ooola may ride Dinny if she can climb aboard.*

convince/persuade. You *convince* someone of something, but you *persuade* someone to do something.

*Dottie can't **persuade** Marmaduke to come because he's **convinced** she wants to give him a bath.*

decimated. Strictly speaking, if something is *decimated,* a tenth of it is wiped out. But almost no one uses *decimated* strictly these days. It's commonly used to mean "destroyed in large part." *Mr. Dithers's layoffs **decimated** the staff.* Just don't use it with a figure (as in ***decimated** by a third*).

dilemma. This isn't merely a problem; it's a predicament with two unpleasant choices. *Archie's **dilemma** was a doozy—either write Moose's term paper or lose a $50 bet.*

disinterested/uninterested. A *disinterested* person is impartial, while an *uninterested* person has no interest at all. *Judge Parker was **disinterested,** and never formed an opinion until the evidence was in. One of the jurors was so **uninterested** in the testimony that he fell asleep.*

e.g./i.e. Don't use these fussy-sounding terms unless you're fussy enough to get them right. The first, *e.g.,* means "for example," and the second, *i.e.,* means "that is." *Daffy has several emotional problems, **e.g.,** a hot temper and delusions of grandeur. He also has a speech impediment, **i.e.,** a lisp.*

emigrate/immigrate. People who leave a place *emigrate* from it—think of *e* for exit—but new arrivals *immigrate* to it. *The Katzenjammers **emigrated** from Germany and eventually **immigrated** to the United States.*

Data Sharing

It's time to face facts. Things change, and *data* has joined *agenda, erotica, insignia, opera,* and other plural Latin or Greek words that have become singular in English. *Flash guessed that the **data** from Ming the Merciless was false.*

Media has come a long way, but it's not quite ready to join *data* and the others. When you're on your best behavior, keep *media* plural. *The news **media** want to interview General Halftrack about the sexual harassment charge.*

English is a living language. Stay tuned for further developments.

---

fewer/less. If you have a smaller number of things, use *fewer.* If you have a smaller amount of one thing, *less* is the word you want. *When Garfield is dieting, he eats **fewer** meals and shares **less** of his kibble with Arlene.*

flaunt/flout. A person who defies or ignores something *flouts* it. One who shows something off *flaunts* it. *Calvin **flouted** Miss Wormwood's dress code when he **flaunted** his baggy pants.*

fortuitous. It means "accidental," not "fortunate" or "lucky." *It was **fortuitous** that Cathy picked the only Zinfandel her friend Irving couldn't stand.*

fulsome. This doesn't mean "lavish" or "flattering"; it

means "sickeningly overdone." *Ignoring Acme's ful-some apologies, Wile E. Coyote sued the company for damages.*

gantlet/gauntlet. Somebody throws down a *gauntlet* but runs a *gantlet*. How come? Because in olden times a fellow threw down a *gauntlet* (a glove) to issue a challenge, while a troublemaker had to run a *gantlet* (a row of guys with switches or clubs) as a form of punishment. *Throwing down the **gauntlet**, Aunt Fritzi declared her candidacy, then ran a **gantlet** of press photographers.*

good/well. When you describe an action, use *well*. When you describe a thing or a condition, use *good* instead. *Morticia looked **good** when her makeup was done **well**.* You can use either *well* or *good* to mean "healthy." *Gomez felt **well** after drinking the potion. "I never felt so **good**," he said.*

graduate. People don't *graduate* Harvard. Harvard *graduates* them. Or they *graduate from* Harvard. Or they *are graduated from* Harvard. *When Bluto **graduated** from barber college, he was asked to shave.*

hero. Some words die out because they're not used enough, others because they're used too much. This one is so overused that it may have lost its meaning. A *hero* is someone who braves great danger for a noble purpose, not someone who manages to pitch a no-hitter or win a bundle on "Who Wants to Be a Millionaire." *It took a **hero** like Wonder Woman to*

All Together Now

What would we do without words like *all, any,* and *every*? For sheer usefulness, they're hard to beat, which is why we use them in so many combinations. But when combinations sound alike—*any way* and *anyway,* for example, or *all together* and *altogether*—how do we tell them apart? Here's the skinny.

all ready/already. Someone who's *all ready* is prepared. *Sluggo is **all ready** to go to the gym.* The short form—note the single *l*—means "previously" or "by now." *He's **already** starting to sweat.*

all right. This is the only form that's all right. "Alright" is wrong, though your spell-checker may be too polite (or too stupid) to tell you. *"The nutritionist didn't say anything about banana cream pie, so it must be **all right**," said Tubby.*

all together/altogether. *All together* means "gathered in one place." *The Munsters were **all together** for Halloween.* But *altogether*—note the single *l*—means "entirely." *They were **altogether** frightening.*

any more/anymore. Use two words, *any more,* when you mean "any additional." *Dennis hasn't broken **any more** windows.* Use one word, *anymore,* when you mean "any longer." *Mr. Wilson doesn't call the police **anymore**.*

any one/anyone. Use one word, *anyone,* if you could substitute "anybody." *Can **anyone** lend*

Aunt Fritzi an umbrella? Otherwise, use *any one,* two words. ***Any one** of them will do.*

any time/anytime. The combined word, *anytime,* means "at any time," but use two words if you mean "any amount of time." *"Call me **anytime** Thursday,"* said Ziggy, *"because I won't have **any time** today."*

any way/anyway. *Any way* is another way of saying "any means." *Is there **any way** of avoiding Rollo's party?* It's one word only if you mean "in any case." *You weren't invited **anyway**.*

every day/everyday. Use two words, *every day,* if you mean "each and every day." *Veronica washes her hair **every day**.* Use one word, *everyday,* as an adjective to mean "ordinary." *Her **everyday** shampoo costs $25 a bottle.*

every one/everyone. If you can substitute "everybody," stick with *everyone,* one word. *Casper alienated **everyone** at the séance.* If not, use two words. *He could see through **every one** of them.*

disarm the nuclear warhead. This may be a lost cause, but try to keep the heroism in *hero* and save it for truly heroic occasions.

historic/historical. Something *historic* has an important place in history, but something *historical* has to do with the subject of history. *Miss Grundy once cracked a joke, but there's no **historical** record of that **historic** moment.*

hopefully. To be literal, *hopefully* means "in a hopeful manner." *"Is the Batmobile fixed?" Robin asked **hopefully**.* But most people use it these days to mean "it is hoped" or "I hope." *"**Hopefully** the Batmobile is fixed," he said.* So what do you do? If you're writing to a stickler, stick to the literal meaning.

imply/infer. To *imply* is to suggest something without actually stating it. To *infer* is to conclude something that wasn't actually stated. *The cop **implied** that the witness committed suicide, or that's what Brenda Starr **inferred** from the arrest report.*

irony. It seems that the more the word *irony* is used, the less it's understood. Now, that's ironic. This is the story. *Irony* is saying one thing when you mean pretty much the opposite. *"What a wonderful Valentine's Day present," Dick Tracy said with **irony** when Tess filed for divorce.* Something is *ironic* when it's the opposite of what you'd expect. *"Isn't it **ironic** that your name is Trueheart?" he said to Tess.*

literally. This means "exactly," "strictly," "word for word." *Baby Skeezix was **literally** left on Walt's doorstep.* Don't confuse it with *figuratively,* which means "metaphorically" or "in an imaginative way." *Walt may have been **figuratively** head over heels in love with Phyllis, but he never **literally** left the ground.*

nauseated/nauseous. Do you want to throw up? Or do you make other people want to throw up? If you're sick to your stomach, you're *nauseated.* If something is sickening (not you, we hope), it's *nauseous*. *Shoe was **nauseated** after drinking the **nauseous** coffee at Roz's Roost.*

rack/wrack. If you're *racked* with guilt, you're tortured, tormented, and punished, like someone on the *rack* in the Dark Ages. If you're *wracked,* you're ruined—you're a wreck. *Clark was **racked** with self-loathing as Lex Luthor and his henchmen **wracked** Gotham.*

stationary/stationery. Writing paper is *stationery*—both include *er*. *Stationary* means "fixed in place," like the laser printer you load with *stationery*. *As Peter Parker rode his **stationary** bicycle, he used Aunt Jane's **stationery** to write a letter to the* Daily Bugle.

than/then. Nope, not the same. Use *than* when you're comparing things. *Tubby is fatter **than** Lulu.* Use *then* when one thing leads to another. *First he goes to Taco Bell, **then** to Baskin-Robbins.* With English, if it isn't one thing, then it's another.

unique. Something *unique* is one of a kind. It's the Colosseum or the Louvre Museum, the Tower of Pisa or the Mona Lisa. In other words, there's nothing like it in this world—or in any other. Nothing can be sort of, rather, or very unique. *Prince Valiant's Singing Sword isn't **unique**; it's the twin of King Arthur's Excalibur.*

13. Alphabet Soup
Spelling It Right

An e-mailer who shall remain nameless is a wretched speller, so wretched that he makes fun of himself by quoting Winnie-the-Pooh in his tag line: "My spelling is Wobbly. It's good spelling but it Wobbles, and the letters get in the wrong places."

If your spelling wobbles too, you're not alone. Many people seem to think spelling doesn't matter anymore, certainly not in e-mail and other online writing. They're the ones who thrive on chaos, who find turmoil and confusion the most endearing qualities of virtual life. Why should they worry about spelling when everything is so open, so accessible, so democratic? They blithely sign on and free-associate. Dictionary? Spell-checker? No, thanks. They like to feel the wind in their hair.

To be sure, these carefree types can usually get their ideas across despite the whimsical spelling. If they want their ideas respected, however, they should treat them with respect. Why bother choosing your words carefully if you don't spell them carefully? You wouldn't wear a grungy T-shirt to a job interview, unless you were auditioning for a role in *Rent*. So clean up your grungy e-mail.

Most people will overlook a typo. But not everyone, and definitely not if every other word is mangled. Some readers will just tune out a message riddled with misspellings. Others may read the message, yet they'll wonder whether the writer's thinking is as sloppy as her spelling. If you're trying to get a point across, particularly when you want to be businesslike, why make trouble?

Don't kid yourself—spelling matters. Search online discussions for the word "spelling" and you'll find thousands of food fights over too many *r*'s, not enough *s*'s, and *i* before *e*—or is it the other way around? We're not necessarily talking about highbrow discussions. No matter what the subject—John Milton or Uncle Miltie, *Howards End* or Howard Stern—people care about spelling.

Most of us would rather spend our time online defending our ideas, not our lousy spelling. Happily, of all the things that separate good writing from bad, spelling is the easiest to do something about. You only have to develop a few good habits.

First, buy a dictionary if you don't already have one, and keep it by the computer when you write. But don't assume that every word in the dictionary is legit. Incorrect spellings (like "alright" or "restauranteur" or "momento") may be listed merely because people use them. Read the fine print!

Second, run whatever you write through the computer's spell-checker before sending it. Now here's the tricky part. Don't mindlessly follow the advice that pops up on the screen. Spell-checkers are terrific, but they're not perfect—ours mistakenly thinks "alright" is all right. If you have any doubts about a word, double-check it. When your dictionary disagrees with the spell-checker, take the dictionary's word for it.

Third, reread everything before sending it. And if it's really important, reread it again. Yes, this is a drag, but we've caught dozens of misspellings at the last minute, and you will too.

Here are the preferred American spellings of some words that spell trouble. When you run across one, even if you think you know how to spell it, a warning buzzer should go off in your mind. Give it another look. If you're not sure, check it out. And if you stumble over an unfamiliar word that's not listed here, look it up in the dictionary—it's there beside your computer, right?

absence. There's no *se* at the end. *"I was fatigued, hence my **absence**,"* Camille said, coughing into her hankie.

access. It has two *c*'s and two *s*'s, as do *accessible* and *accessibility. "Without a password, I don't have **access** to the classified files,"* Smiley complained.

accidentally. Some people spell this word as if it had only four syllables, "accidently." But think of the root as *accidental,* then add the final *ly. Britney ruined her pedicure when she **accidentally** dropped the mike.*

Weird Species

In grade school, we memorized a little rhyme that still comes in handy: "*i* before *e,* except after *c.*" Say what you will about rote memorization, that old rhyme has bailed us out of many a spelling difficulty over the years. Even though it doesn't work one hundred percent of the time, it's a good place to start when you're spelling a word in which *e* and *i* (or *i* and *e*) come together.

The words that give us trouble are the exceptions to the "*i* before *e*" rule. Some of them, as it happens, have a rule of their own:

• Use *e* before *i* when the letters rhyme with "hay": *aweigh, eighth, freight, neigh, neighbor, rein, surveillance, weigh.*

Sorry, but you'll just have to memorize the other exceptions: *either, financier, foreign, forfeit, height, leisure, neither, seize, sheik, sovereign, species, surfeit, weird.*

---

accommodate. The two *c*'s and two *m*'s trip people up. *"I'm afraid we cannot **accommodate** a table of twenty,"* the headwaiter told the Bradys.

The Check Is in the Mail

When you have a few minutes to spare, try searching the Web for the word "cirrocumuli." As expected, you'll find these high-altitude clouds mentioned on numerous meteorological sites. But you'll also see them on dozens of academic pages that have nothing to do with weather. What gives?

It just so happens that some computer spell-checkers suggest "cirrocumuli" as an alternative if you misspell "curriculum." And a lot of trusting souls, even educators who should know better, simply hit Replace when their software recommends another word.

If to err is human, spell-checkers must surely be one of us. In fact, they've inspired a new art form, nonsense verse that shows how very human spell-checkers can be. You'll never trust your speller again after it gives one of these rhymes a passing grade. The most famous example (there are countless variations) begins:

> *I have a spelling checker*
> *It came with my pea see*
> *It plane lee marks four my revue*
> *Miss steaks eye can knot sea.*

Another creative way to waste time online is to play name games with your spell-checker. That's when you feed in a name the software doesn't recognize, and see what alternatives are suggested.

Ours thinks Judi Dench should call herself Drench
and Denzel Washington ought to be Densely.

By all means use your spell-checker, but don't
blindly follow its advice. If you're not sure that a
suggestion is okay, look it up in the dictionary.

Incidentally, don't add words to your spelling
software unless you're certain they're correct. It's
much easier to add a word than to subtract one. If
you've ever tried to lose a few pounds, you know
what we're talking about.

In chapter 11, we ran a speech by Bill Gates
through the Microsoft Word grammar-checker. In
the interest of fairness, we tried out AOL's spell-
checker on a speech by Steve Case. As you might
suspect, it made a lot of dumb suggestions, like replacing "don't" with "donut," "diasporas" with "dis-
appear," and "Euros" with "Eurasia." To top it off,
AOL's speller didn't recognize "e-commerce."

---

achievement. As if the *ie* issue weren't enough,
achieve keeps its final *e* when *ment* is added. *"Ten
hot dogs in thirty seconds is a spectacular **achievement**," Moose bragged.*

acknowledgment. Don't forget the *d,* and remember
that *acknowledge* loses its final *e* when *ment* is
added. *After weeks of work organizing the benefit,
Isaac got only a tiny **acknowledgment** in the program.*

acquaintance. Make sure there's a *c* before the *q*.

"*Pleased to make your* **acquaintance**, *I'm sure,"* said *Dr. Livingstone.*

advertise. There's no *z*. *"What was I supposed to do,* **advertise** *in the personals?" Darva asked.*

advisable. It ends in *able*, not *ible*. *"Playing with matches is not* **advisable**," *warned Brenda the firefighter.*

aficionado. Only one *f*. *"Are you a cigar* **aficionado**, *too?" Fidel asked.*

aging. No *e*. *Say what you will about Dorian, he's* **aging** *beautifully.*

all right. It's two words (not "alright"). *"**All right**, I'll go quietly!" said Puffy.*

a lot. No, not "alot," though a lot of online writers think otherwise. *"That's* **a lot** *of hooey," said Miss Grundy.*

altar. If you mean the one in church, there's no *e*. *Michael was an* **altar** *boy before he became a don.*

appall. Note the two *p*'s and two *l*'s. *"Those puny stones* **appall** *me, darling," said Zsa Zsa.*

arctic. Don't forget that it has two *c*'s. *"The water is positively* **arctic**," *said Esther, emerging from the Channel.* The place up north is the *Arctic*.

artifact. There's no *e*. *Eddie was an* **artifact** *of Liz's youth.*

battalion. Two *t*'s, but only one *l*. *After a week of R&R, the* **battalion** *ran out of penicillin.*

belief. When *i*'s and *e*'s come together, spelling sometimes comes apart. In this case, the *i* comes before the *e*. *It was Lord Darlington's* **belief** *that the butler did it.*

benefited. *Benefit* is one of those words that don't double the *t* when you add *ed.* *"I never **benefited** from insider information," Ivan insisted.*

buses. There's no double *s* in the middle. *"Max, what are all those **buses** doing in the yard?" Mrs. Yasgur asked.*

canvas. One *s* at the end, unless you mean the kind of *canvass* that's a survey. *"The world is my **canvas**," said Christo.*

capital. The odds are, there's no *o* (a *capitol* is a building where lawmakers meet). *Is Pierre the **capital** of North or South Dakota?*

Surprise Endings

Is a glue stick *eatable,* or is it *edible?* Actually, both words are correct. As for whether it's *palatable*—ask a five-year-old.

Word endings in English can be as strange as children's tastes (we prefer library paste ourselves). Take the many words ending in *able* and *ible.* The only way to get them right is to memorize them or look them up.

The *able*s far outnumber the *ible*s, but some very familiar words are in the minority: *combustible, compatible, credible, deductible, digestible, flexible, irresistible, possible, reprehensible, sensible,* and *susceptible,* among others. As for the indispensable *able*s, there are so many that it's not advisable to list them.

When you're not sure, grab the dictionary.

Icky Solutions

Most of us overdose on politics at election time, but in Washington the politicking never stops. *Politicking* is a funny-looking word, isn't it? As a member of the body politic, have you ever wondered where the *k* comes from?

If a word ends in *c,* we often slip in a *k* to keep the sound "hard" when adding another ending (for instance, *ed, er, ing,* or *y*). Without the *k,* a word like *colicky* would rhyme with *policy.* Here are some other *icky* examples (they aren't as hard as they sound).

bivouac: bivouacked, bivouacking
frolic: frolicked, frolicker, frolicking
garlic: garlicky
mimic: mimicked, mimicking
panic: panicked, panicking, panicky
picnic: picnicked, picnicker, picnicking
shellac: shellacked, shellacking
traffic: trafficked, trafficker, trafficking

---

cemetery. Count 'em—three *e*'s. *"This place is about as exciting as a **cemetery,**" said Lestat.*

commitment. The root word, *commit,* has double *m*'s and only one *t*. *"You're too neurotic to make a **commitment,**" Dr. Laura sneered.*

compatible. It ends in *ible,* not *able*. *Don and Steve can e-mail each other even though their computers aren't **compatible**.*

complexion. Watch out for the unusual *xion* ending. *"Must be the cucumber milk," Uma said, admiring her complexion.*

concede. The *cede* ending is the hard part. *"I'll concede when I'm good and ready, so don't get snippy about it," Al snapped.*

conceive. The *e* comes before the *i*. *"I can't conceive why he divorced me," said Catherine, packing to go back to Spain.*

connoisseur. Two *n*'s and two *s*'s. *Frasier may be a connoisseur, but Niles knows more about Gewürztraminers.*

consensus. The only *c* is at the front. *The consensus on the island was that Richard had to go.*

The Bad Seed

In English, many words sound as if they end in "seed," but unless they have something to do with horticulture they can be pretty confusing. How do you know whether these words end in *cede, ceed,* or *sede*? You can always look them up, of course. Or you can learn a few simple rules for telling the "seeds" apart.

- Only one ends in *sede*: *supersede*.
- Only three end in *ceed*: *exceed, proceed, succeed*.
- All the rest end in *cede*: *accede, concede, intercede, precede, recede, secede*, and others.

credible. The ending is *ible,* not *able. Lypsinka's Joan Crawford is terrific, but her Lucille Ball is barely* **credible.**

deceive. Again, *e* before *i. Mrs. Hudson's flimsy tissue of lies did not* **deceive** *Holmes.*

deductible. A common *ible* word, especially in April. *Leona felt that collagen injections should be* **deductible.**

defense. No *c.* "*The best* **defense** *is a good offense,*" *O.J. said.*

descendant. It ends in *ant,* not *ent. The DNA showed that she was a* **descendant** *of Jefferson.*

desiccated. One *s* and two *c*'s, not the other way around. *After an hour by the pool with no moisturizer, Kathie Lee's skin was* **desiccated.**

desirable. No *e* in the middle. *Groucho wouldn't join any club that found him* **desirable.**

dessert. Two *s*'s, if you're talking about food. "*Sorry, I don't do* **dessert,**" *Amber said, rushing off to a shoot.*

ecstasy. It's the *sy* at the end that causes trouble. *The marquis went to great pains to arrive at* **ecstasy.**

embarrass. Unlike *harass,* this has two *r*'s as well as two *s*'s. *Public displays of affection* **embarrass** *the royals.*

entrepreneur. So many *e*'s and *r*'s! *Pablo was part artist and part* **entrepreneur.**

exhilarate. Don't be tricked by the *h. The atmosphere at Manderley did not* **exhilarate** *Mrs. de Winter.*

eyeing. Keep the second *e. Alice was* **eyeing** *Mr. Dodgson suspiciously.*

fiery. Sounds like *fire*, but it's not spelled that way. *Dr. Dre has a fiery temper.*

flexible. Another *ible* ending. *Mae isn't free, but she's flexible.*

foresee. Don't forget the *e* in the middle. *Nancy's astrologer didn't foresee the collapse of the Soviet Union.*

forfeit. Here, *e* comes before *i*. *Dick vowed to forfeit his stock options if he became vice-president.*

forgo. It means "to do without," and there's no *e*. (*Forgo* is not the same as *forego*, which means "to go before" and is the root of *foregone* and *foregoing*.) *It was a foregone conclusion that Brad and Jennifer would forgo a church wedding.*

forward. No *e*. (Don't confuse it with *foreword*, which is part of a book.) *Norman looked forward to writing the foreword to Germaine's book.*

fuchsia. If you can spell this one without looking it up, you're good. *Bertie's fuchsia cummerbund was from Comme des Garçons.*

fulfill. It's the *l*'s that trip us up: one in the middle and two at the end. *Stephen's e-book didn't fulfill its promise.*

gauge. Get the *u* in the right place. *Maidenform failed to gauge the impact of falling necklines on sales of push-up bras.*

graffiti. Two *f*'s, one *t*. *When the mayor cracked down on graffiti, Jean-Michel saw the writing on the wall.*

grammar. If you end it with *er*, go stand in the corner. *Kelsey's grammar is irreproachable.*

guarantee. It's *ua*, not *au*. *Symantec won't* **guarantee** *that the beta version is free of bugs.*

harass. There's only one *r*. *He didn't want to* **harass** *Gloria, just flirt a little.*

inoculate. Don't be tempted to toss in a second *n* or *c*. *It's too bad Jonas never developed a vaccine to* **inoculate** *people against stupidity.*

intercede. Note the *cede* ending. *Uncle Junior tried to bribe Judge Judy to* **intercede** *on his behalf.*

irresistible. Resist the temptation to end it *able*. *Dr. Lecter found braised liver* **irresistible.**

judgment. The British stick an extra *e* in the middle, but Americans don't. *Julia relied more on her* **judgment** *than her measuring cup.*

knowledge. Remember that the first part spells "know," and don't forget the *d*. *"To the best of my* **knowledge,"** *Albert said, "it's all relative."*

liaison. It takes two *i*'s to make a *liaison*. *"This* **liaison** *is becoming dangerous," Valmont thought.*

liquefy. The troublesome part is the *e*. *"I'm melting!" the witch cried as she began to* **liquefy.**

marshal. One *l*. *Stormin' Norman ordered the colonel to* **marshal** *his troops.* But it's *martial* law when the troops take charge.

marvelous. One *l* again, unless you're British. *Billy still looks* **marvelous.**

memento. It starts with *me* (as in *memory*), not *mo*. *The condo was a* **memento** *of Ivana's marriage.*

millennium. Two *l*'s and two *n*'s. *Martha bought a new glue gun for the **millennium**.*

minuscule. Remember that it starts with *minus,* not *mini. The audience at the Cocteau revival was **minuscule**.*

mischievous. Go easy on the *i*'s—there are only two. *A **mischievous** hacker changed everyone's grades to A's.*

necessary. One *c,* two *s*'s. *Jacques considered lard a **necessary** evil.*

niece. The *i* comes before the *e. Fanny was Jane's favorite **niece**.*

noticeable. Don't forget the *e* in the middle. *Cokie assured him the toupee wasn't **noticeable**.*

nuclear. Only one *u,* so pronounce it that way (not NOO-kyoo-lar). *The **nuclear** family, as well as the atom, was split in the twentieth century.*

occasionally. Two *c*'s, but only one *s. Sandra **occasionally** dresses like a fashionista.*

occur. It starts out with a single *r,* but gains one in *occurrence, occurred,* and *occurring. It didn't **occur** to Plácido to take the A train.*

parallel. The only double letters are the *l*'s in the middle. *Nadia fell off the **parallel** bars.*

pastime. No double letters. *Skateboarding is Lady Thatcher's favorite **pastime**.*

perceive. The *e* comes before the *i. Harold could **perceive** that the lighting was too theatrical.*

Philippines. The only double letters are those *p*'s

inside. *Imelda bought up every last Manolo slingback in the **Philippines**.*

pneumonia. Don't let the *p* throw you. *Kate had a sinking feeling that she'd come down with **pneumonia**.*

Portuguese. There's a second *u*. *Elizabeth's favorite sonnets were from the **Portuguese**.*

prairie. There are two *i*'s. *Roy liked to sing to Trigger on the lone **prairie**.*

precede. Note the *cede* ending. *Ralph wanted his fall show to **precede** Calvin's.*

pretensions. The *sion* is what leads people astray. *The salad bar at Pizza Hut had no **pretensions**.*

principle. Its meaning is similar to "rule" or "belief." (The word ending in *al, principal,* refers to an important person or thing, such as a financial holding.) *Principal Harper is opposed on **principle** to sex in the broom closets.*

privilege. Two *i*'s come first, then two *e*'s. *"It's a **privilege** to meet you," said Stanley.*

proceed. This is one of the few words that end in *ceed*. *Dr. Barnard couldn't **proceed** without a donor.*

publicly. It doesn't end in *ally*. *The duchess was **publicly** humiliated by the photos.*

pursue. No *per* at the beginning. *The stalker used computer data banks to **pursue** Rebecca.*

questionnaire. Unlike *millionaire* and *billionaire*, this has a double *n*. *Donald asked prospective dates to fill out a **questionnaire**.*

rarefied. Appropriately, it begins with *rare*. *Brooke considered herself a woman of **rarefied** tastes.*

receive. The *c* is a hint that *e* comes before *i*. *The tight end wasn't supposed to **receive** the pass.*

recommend. One *c*, two *m*'s. *"I **recommend** that you wake up and smell the coffee," said Ann.*

regardless. No, it does not start with *i*, as in "irregardless." *Big Julie always bet on the underdog, **regardless** of the odds.*

reminisce. Words with *sc* are easy to misspell. *Marcel liked to **reminisce** about pastry.*

renaissance. Double *s*, but only one *n* at a time. *Suddenly there was a **renaissance** in Bob and Elizabeth's love life.*

restaurateur. There's no *n*! *Pierre loved to cook, but he didn't want to be a **restaurateur**.*

sacrilegious. It doesn't include the word "religious" (think "sacrilege" instead). *Mae is irreverent, but she's not **sacrilegious**.*

scissors. Wow—four *s*'s, one at each end and a pair in the middle. *Coco asked the seamstress for a pair of **scissors**.*

seize. Again, *e* before *i*. *Evita would **seize** any opportunity to help Juan.*

sensible. The ending is *ible*, not *able*. *Miss Marple wore a tweed suit and **sensible** shoes.*

separate. The second vowel is *a*, not *e*. *Dennis and Meg sat at **separate** tables.*

sergeant. Despite the pronunciation, it doesn't start

A Full House

Hackers like to use creative spellings—some even call themselves "haquors." It's their way of subverting the language and driving authority figures crazy. But if you'd rather please the authority figures in your life—or if you're an authority figure yourself—it's better to use conventional spellings.

You can usually tell an authoritative speller by the way she handles tricky words, and some of the trickiest contain *ful* or *full*. Even good spellers go to the dictionary (one *l* or two?) when faced with these full-bodied words.

If the tricky part comes last, the word ends in one *l*. A useful rule of thumb, don't you think? Familiar examples include *armful, awful, careful, cupful, graceful, hopeful, houseful, meaningful, peaceful, playful, sinful, spoonful, useful, watchful, wonderful*. (But when you add an *ly* ending to words like these, keep both *l*'s: *carefully, playfully, wonderfully,* and so on.)

The odds are pretty good that if the tricky part comes first, it's also spelled with only one *l*: *fulcrum, fulfill, fulminate, fulsome*. (Exceptions are *fullness* and *fullback*.)

Don't be flummoxed by plural forms like *armfuls, bucketfuls, handfuls, mouthfuls,* and *spoonfuls*. Strange as it may seem, people carrying cups full of coffee are carrying *cupfuls* of coffee. English is full of wonders.

> When *full* is a separate word, even if it's connected to another word with a hyphen, use two *l*'s: *full-blown, full-dress, full-time, full-service, full-size.* (There's more about hyphens, and when to use them, in the next chapter.) That's the full story.

with "sarge." *The **sergeant** at arms told Tom and Trent to stop biting each other.*

siege. A clear case of *i* before *e*. *Zelda was under **siege** by hordes of suitors.*

skillful. Two *l*'s in the middle, but only one at the end. *"A woman like Katharina requires **skillful** handling," Petruchio said.*

sprightly. It has *right* in the middle. (Not *spritely*, unless you're talking about elves or gnomes.) *Grandma Moses was a **sprightly** newcomer on the art scene.*

straitlaced. There's no *straight* in *straitlaced* (think of a narrow *strait*). *The only thing **straitlaced** about Madonna was her bustier.*

subtly. *Subtle* loses its *e* when it becomes *subtly* (but it keeps the *e* in *subtlety*). *Zelig **subtly** transformed himself into someone not known for subtlety.*

succeed. Two *c*'s and two *e*'s. *The Cardinals didn't **succeed** in signing Sammy.*

supersede. Here it is, the only English word ending in *sede*. *Does Rupert think the e-book will **supersede** the real thing?*

surveillance. Two *l*'s, as in "intelligence." *French intelligence agents had Carlos under* **surveillance**.

susceptible. The *c* gives people problems, as does the *ible* ending. *Oscar was* **susceptible** *to Bosie's charms*.

temperament. Don't forget the *a*. *Josephine had the right* **temperament** *for a dancer*.

tranquillity. The preferred spelling has two *l*'s (unlike "tranquilizer"), and if your spell-checker says otherwise, it's wrong. *Paul's blackened redfish was a recipe for* **tranquillity**.

unnecessary. Double *n* and double *s,* but only one *c*. *Buzz wasn't allowed to take any* **unnecessary** *luggage*.

unwieldy. Only one *l* (the ending isn't *ly*). *Dr. Ruth found the Hummer* **unwieldy** *in the parking lot*.

weird. This time, *e* before *i*. *Everything tastes* **weird** *to Calista*.

wholly. Two *l*'s. *Jerry believes the Holy Bible to be* **wholly** *true*.

yield. The *i* comes first. *Mario refused to* **yield** *the lead to A.J.*

14. Period Piece
The Perils of Punctuation

Pat groans whenever she has to spell her last name over the phone. "O-apostrophe-C-O-N-N-E-R," she says, and invariably the person at the other end responds, "O-what?" Just try explaining to the voice at the power company or the hair salon what that little thingy is between the O and the C. Even their Web sites may not recognize an apostrophe when a customer fills in her name.

What's happened to the apostrophe? For that matter, what's happened to the comma, the period, and all the other punctuation marks? Offline, they're abused mercilessly. Online, they're hardly ever used (except for dashes and exclamation points, which are to online writing what French fries are to McDonald's).

It hasn't helped that those cutesy emoticons people use online are tiny pictures made of punctuation marks. After a while, folks start thinking of hyphens as noses, parentheses as smiles or frowns, colons as eyes (and semicolons as winks).

But punctuation marks aren't just facial expressions, and they're about as cutesy as those green, red, and yellow traffic lights that make driving such a colorful experience. Reading something without punctuation is like driving without traffic signals. You can do it, of course, but you're more likely to get where you're going—and in one piece—with some directions along the way.

Punctuation has taken a beating in the age of e-mail. We know plenty of writers and editors who are meticulous about commas, quotation marks, and such in "real" writing. Their e-mail is another matter. One uses no punctuation at all other than periods (no capital letters, either), while another can't stop. ("Punctuation adds so much expression!!!! I mean, it's supposed to be fun, right???!") These two should be introduced to the concept of the happy medium.

For sheer readability, few things make as much difference as punctuation marks. And the seconds it takes you to add them can save wear and tear on the reader. Besides, they don't cost you anything. You're not being charged by the comma.

Punctuation was invented to help writing make sense, and online writing needs as much help as any other. Maybe more. A hurried, breezy, spontaneous message is easy to misunderstand. Punctuation slows the rush of words, breaking them up into smaller groups that are easier to grasp. Without punctuation, the reader is forced to supply the pauses and stops and slight hesitations and new beginnings.

Imagine an e-mail like this: *Stacey insisted Steve fired the director.* As it reads now, Steve did the firing. But insert a couple of commas and Stacey becomes the heavy: *Stacey, insisted Steve, fired the director.*

If you still don't think punctuation matters, figure this one out: *Who got fired Stacey said the director.* Here are a few possibilities.

> *"Who got fired, Stacey?" said the director.*
> *Who got fired? Stacey, said the director.*
> *Who got fired? Stacey said the director.*

It doesn't take long to add those little marks, but what a difference they make! Now for a refresher course on how they work.

The Periodic Table

When a plain, straightforward sentence like this one is over, it ends with a dot. We call the dot a period (from a Greek word indicating "period of time") because it shows that the sentence has come to an end—that is, its period is up.

Sometimes, when words are abbreviated (as in 3 P.M. or T. J. Eckleburg or Babbitt-Thompson Realty Co.), they get periods, too, though the trend these days is to drop the dots in many abbreviations (MD, CEO, and CPA, for instance). Check your dictionary for the latest.

Most of the time, you don't have to worry about periods. Once in a while, though, you'll arrive at the end of a sentence only to find a punctuation mark there already. Do you need the period, too? If so, does it go before or after what's already there? Here are some points to consider.

- If a sentence ends with a dotted abbreviation, don't add another dot. (A sentence can't end with two dots in a row—three or four occasionally, but never just two.) *Mrs. Eckleburg always called her son Thaddeus Jedidiah, not T.J.*

- If a sentence ends with the title of a book or movie or the like, and that title has a question mark or an exclamation point at the end, don't add a period. *Dr. Eckleburg's favorite movie was* Help! *His favorite book was* Why Do Clocks Run Clockwise?

- If a large sentence includes a smaller one surrounded by dashes or parentheses, don't use a period after the "inside" sentence. *Dr. Eckleburg's parting remark—"You'd look great in contacts"— was the same with every bespectacled patient.* If the inside sentence is a question or exclamation, keep the punctuation. *His opinion of laser surgery ("Laser, shmaser! Why bother?") was a familiar refrain.*

- If a sentence ends with an ellipsis (an omission, indicated by three dots), put in a period first. *To Dr. Eckleburg, the bottom line meant only one thing: P, E, Z, O. . . .* But if you want to emphasize that a sentence is deliberately left hanging, use only the three dots. *As Dorothy left Dr. Eckleburg's office, she had a thought. Men seldom make passes at girls who . . .*

- If a sentence ends with an aside in parentheses, the period goes outside. *Dr. Eckleburg recommended eye exams once a year (twice if the insurer would cover them).* But if an entire sentence is in parentheses, the period goes inside. *Two checkups a year are ideal, he said. (He knew, though, that most insurers covered only one.)*

- If a sentence ends with a quotation, put the period inside the quotation marks. *Dr. Eckleburg put down the novel after reading the last words: "So we beat on, boats against the current, borne back ceaselessly into the past."*

Comma Knowledge

The words "comma" and "comedy" have little in common except for their first three letters. Or so you'd think. If you have some time to kill, visit a few humor sites on the Internet and see how many jokes revolve around commas and other punctuation. One of our favorite examples is a letter that's punctuated two different ways.

Here's one version:

Dear John: I want a man who knows what love is all about. You are generous, kind, thoughtful. People who are not like you admit to being useless and inferior. You have ruined me for other men. I yearn for you. I have no feelings whatsoever when we're apart. I can be forever happy—will you let me be yours? Gloria.

Here's the other:

Dear John: I want a man who knows what love is. All about you are generous, kind, thoughtful people, who are not like you. Admit to being useless and inferior. You have ruined me. For other men, I yearn. For you, I have no feelings whatsoever. When we're apart, I can be forever happy. Will you let me be? Yours, Gloria.

Notice how a few extra commas and other punctuation marks can make the difference between a kiss and a kiss-off. Without punctuation, a string of words could mean many different things—most of them unintended.

To make sense, words have to be arranged in groups. This is where punctuation comes in. And when it comes to making arrangements, the comma may be the best of the bunch.

The term "comma" comes from a Greek word meaning "to cut," and that's exactly what a comma does. It cuts a sentence into smaller pieces, organizing words into groups that mean one thing rather than another. Sometimes the difference can turn a sentence upside down, as in these two: *John insisted Gloria was a jerk. John, insisted Gloria, was a jerk.*

Anyone can learn to use this punctuation mark correctly. Simply follow these steps and develop the comma touch.

- Use commas to separate clauses (a clause is a part of a sentence with its own subject and verb). *John had forgotten her birthday five times in a row, but Gloria thought this year would be different.*
- Use commas between items in a list. *Gloria was hoping for dinner, dancing, and flowers. She was furious to learn that John hadn't made a dinner reservation, called the florist, or even bought a card.*
- Use commas before or after a quotation. *Gloria said, "I might have known." "I'll make it up to you somehow," John promised.* (The comma always comes ahead of the final quote marks.) But don't use a comma after a quotation that's a question or an exclamation. *"Why not kiss and make up?" John asked.*
- Use commas before or after the name of someone being addressed. *"Gloria, you're overreacting," he said. "Maybe you're right, John," she answered.*
- Use a comma after an introductory remark if you want to emphasize the pause. *Fortunately, the argument was soon over. Before long, they were cuddling on the couch.*

- Use commas around an aside, as you might use dashes or parentheses. *He dialed Chez Panisse, their favorite restaurant, and managed to wangle a reservation for that night.*
- Use commas around a clause that interrupts a sentence to insert a thought. These interruptions usually begin with *which, where, who,* or *when. They arrived at Chez Panisse, which was half an hour away, at ten. The waiter, who knew John and Gloria, joined them in a toast.* Don't use a comma if there's no interruption. *John knew which wine was which. Gloria knew when she was ahead.*

Exclaim Check

Have you noticed the epidemic of exclamation points in cyberspace? Take the Web site that touted itself as "the Internet's most exciting real money on-line casino." Just to make sure you realized how exciting it was, the designers of the gambling site named it !!!Casino!!!

Why do people think they can spice up a bland message by slopping on punctuation like salsa? The only thing you achieve by adding exclamation points to humdrum writing is to show how humdrum the writing really is. Instead, try adding excitement to the words themselves. Then, if you still feel the need for exclamation points, use them sparingly and make sure you get them right. This is how.

- Use exclamation points one at a time, please. *Alfredo's gambling his life away for Violetta!*

- Use either an exclamation point or a question mark, but never both. *Surely he isn't at the gaming table again!* Or, *Surely he isn't at the gaming table again?*

- Use an exclamation point within quotation marks if the exclamation is what's being quoted. *"Deal the cards!"* Don't add a comma after the exclamation if the sentence continues. *"Hurry up!" he shouted.*

- Use an exclamation point outside quotation marks if the whole sentence, not just the quote, is an exclamation. *Uh-oh, Alfredo's father just called Violetta a "floozy"!*

- Use an exclamation point outside parentheses if the whole sentence, not just the aside, is an exclamation. *Quick, get the doctor (she's coughing again)!*

- Use an exclamation point within parentheses if only the aside, not the whole sentence, is an exclamation. *Violetta died in his arms (how she suffered!).* Note that the period goes last.

Out of the Question

We were lurking on a Mac discussion board when we noticed this message from a guy who claimed to have patented the question mark: "Any use of the symbol '?' is a patent infringement. I will litigate until I have been properly compensated for my investment, toil, and marketing efforts on this ingenious invention. If you have any questions, you'll have to figure something else out. Sorry."

He was only kidding, naturally. But think about it. Imagine a world without question marks. It would be a pretty dull place, wouldn't it? Even e-mail junkies who can't be bothered with periods or commas never tire of question marks. If anything, they use too many.

Why? Maybe because the question mark is so expressive. You can almost hear a question mark, that rising inflection universally recognized as "Huh?" You can almost see the writer's raised eyebrows. No wonder question marks are so popular. Online writing needs all the expressiveness it can get.

Nine times out of ten, there's no question about how to use a question mark. But what about those questionable times? We thought you'd never ask.

- Use only one at a time. *Kinsey was puzzled. How did Rizzo's body get in the dumpster?* (Not: *How did Rizzo's body get in the dumpster???*)
- Don't use them with exclamation points. *With Koko at the groomer and Yum Yum at the vet, how was Qwilleran supposed to solve the case?* (Not: *With Koko at the groomer and Yum Yum at the vet, how was Qwilleran supposed to solve the case!?!?*)
- If a sentence is a series of questions, put the question mark at the end. *Was Kay looking at a drowning, a shooting, a stabbing, or all of the above?* (If you

prefer, make each a separate question. *Was Kay looking at a drowning? A shooting? A stabbing? Or all of the above?*)

- If a question is part of a larger sentence, put the question mark immediately after the question. *When would the threatening phone calls stop? wondered Alex.*
- If an entire question is a quotation, the question mark goes inside the quotation marks. *"How can you get fingerprints off someone with no hands?" asked Vic.*
- If only part of a question is a quotation, the question mark goes outside the quote marks. *How did Ezekiel get the nickname "Easy"?*
- If an entire question is in parentheses, the question mark goes inside. *(How could Chee and Leaphorn forget to read him his rights?)*
- If only part of a question is in parentheses, the question mark goes outside. *How many cases did Peter solve last month (not counting the one Rina helped with)?*

Colon Cards

Stewart wanted to begin this discussion of the colon with a joke about intestinal fortitude, but Pat's cooler head prevailed. So, if we can put aside the bathroom humor, just what does this punctuation mark do?

This is what: It introduces something, like a quotation, a statement, or a list of things. For further instructions, read on:

- Use a colon instead of a comma to introduce a long quotation or one with several sentences. *Willy said: "They don't need me in New York. I'm the New England man. I'm vital in New England."*

- Use a colon to introduce a series of things. *Willy's territory included three key cities: Boston, Providence, and Portland.* (The intro should be a clause, a group of words with its own subject and verb.)

- Don't use a colon to separate the verb from the things it introduces, as in this example. *Willy's territory included: Boston, Providence, and Portland.* Instead, drop the colon. *Willy's territory included Boston, Providence, and Portland.*

- Use a colon to introduce a set of instructions. *The directions to the Wagner plant are easy: left on Maple, right on Sixth Street, then left at the second light.*

- Use a colon to introduce a statement or a conclusion. *Willy's wife sensed the truth: he was burned out.* (The second part doesn't have to be a complete sentence. *To Linda, the answer was obvious: clinical depression.*)

- Use a capital letter after the colon if the second part is a complete sentence and you want to emphasize it. *Biff's advice to Willy was simple: Get help.*

Semiliterate

A company in Silicon Valley came up with a logo that would warm the hearts of many a punctuation lover. The design, a road winding upward in a graceful curve toward the sun, forms a large semicolon. The company's name? Semicolon Software.

It's fitting that a producer of game software would use the semicolon in such a creative way. E-mailers and other online writers may not use this punctuation mark much (except in emoticons), but programmers practically wear it out.

Software writers use the semicolon to put several programming commands on the same line. We mere mortals, who write for people and not for machines, use the semicolon in much the same way—to separate clauses or items in a complicated series. (A clause, you'll recall, is part of a sentence with its own subject and verb.)

If you rarely use semicolons in your online writing, do reconsider. This underappreciated punctuation mark is much simpler than it looks, and it can do wonders to organize a messy sentence or paragraph. If you're only semi-convinced, keep an open mind.

- Use a semicolon to separate clauses that aren't joined by "and" or another connecting word. *Leontyne enjoys the Beastie Boys; Cecilia fancies Nine Inch Nails.* (Each clause could be a sentence in itself, but the result would be choppier.)
- Use semicolons to separate a series when some of the items already have commas inside them. *Wendy's musical tastes include jazz, especially bebop;*

goth; Couperin, when she's in a Baroque mood; polka; and post-grunge, mostly Foo Fighters. (That would be a confusing mishmash if it had only commas.)

The semicolon's an acquired taste, like caviar, snails, or library paste.

In Loco Parenthesis

Remember Mr. Micawber, the long-winded debtor from *David Copperfield*? He can't discuss his prospects without throwing in an aside about how something will turn up (of which he's rather confident) and change his fortunes (in fact, he's hourly expecting it).

Using asides in parentheses doesn't necessarily make you a windbag. It's a handy way to interrupt yourself without losing your way. The only problem with parentheses is how to use them with other punctuation marks. Do the other marks go inside or out?

- If the aside is a separate sentence, the punctuation mark at the end goes inside the parentheses. *"My dear Copperfield," said Mr. Micawber. (He treated young David like an adult.)*
- If the aside is only part of a sentence, any punctuation marks dividing or ending the sentence go outside the parentheses. *Mr. Micawber was a man of some experience (as he liked to say), and he believed that procrastination was the thief of time (he was in a position to know).*

- If the aside is a question, an exclamation, or a quotation, then the question mark, exclamation point, or quotation marks go inside the parentheses. *Despite Mrs. Micawber's burdens (was any wretch so miserable?), she stood by her husband (what devotion!) and always would ("I won't desert Mr. Micawber").* Again, the marks dividing and ending the sentence stay outside the parentheses.

One more aside. If you use a lot of smileys in your online writing, go easy on the parentheses. Try dashes instead.

Quote Couture

What's your favorite quotation? The beginning of *Anna Karenina*? The last line of *Gone With the Wind*? Something Marvin Gaye heard through the grapevine? Or Blanche DuBois's finding Stanley Kowalski a little bit on the, uh, primitive side?

Everybody has a favorite quote. Look how many people use them in their e-mail signatures. When you use a quotation in your writing, starting it is no hassle. Just put the opening quotation marks right in front of the first quoted word. The dicey part is at the end of the quote. Where do you put the other punctuation marks you'll be using, the periods and commas and such—inside or outside the closing quotation marks?

Not many movies are as quotable as *Casablanca,*

so let's stop by Rick's Café Américain for an apéritif and a few examples of quotation marks at work. You must remember this.

- Periods and commas always go inside quotation marks. *"I came to Casablanca for the waters," Rick said. "I was misinformed."*
- Colons and semicolons always go outside quotation marks. *Louis told Strasser the climate was "a trifle warm"; two German couriers had been killed. The police were rounding up "twice the usual number of suspects": black marketeers, smugglers, pickpockets, and so on.*
- A question mark goes inside quotation marks if the question itself is what's being quoted. *"Why did you have to come to Casablanca?" Rick asked Ilsa.* But a question mark goes outside quotation marks if it's not part of the quotation. *And why did she ask Sam to play "As Time Goes By"?*
- An exclamation point goes inside quotation marks if the exclamation itself is what's being quoted. *"I'm shocked, shocked to find that gambling is going on in here!" Louis said, then collected his winnings.* But an exclamation point goes outside quotation marks if it's not part of the quotation. *He had the nerve to call himself "a poor, corrupt official"!*
- Parentheses go outside quotation marks if the quotation is within a parenthetical aside. *Rick remembered every detail. ("The Germans wore gray. You*

wore blue.") But parentheses go inside quotation marks if the parenthetical aside is within a quotation. *"Yes," Ilsa said. "I put that dress away. (When the Germans march out I'll wear it again.)"*

- Single quotation marks go around a quote that's part of a larger quotation. *"I'm not fighting for anything anymore except myself," Rick said. "I'm the only 'cause' I'm interested in."*

When you use quotation marks, the fundamental things apply. The words inside those marks aren't just words; they're exact words. Quote people honestly and accurately. If you don't, you'll damage your own reputation more than anyone else's. On that you can rely. So get to know quotation marks. It could be the beginning of a beautiful friendship.

Dash Bored

Dashes haven't been this popular since Victorian times, when a hasty dash of the pen was a genteel substitute for an unmentionable word like "damn" or "hell" or "devil." Nowadays, online writers don't use dashes to say the unsayable—they use them to write the unreadable.

Don't misunderstand. Dashes, like other punctuation marks, are fine when used in moderation. Think of them as detours in a sentence. They let you leave the main road, explore an interesting byway, then resume your trip.

But many online writers don't use dashes in moderation. They stick in a dash here, a dash there, dashes everywhere. The result is jerky writing that's hard to read.

Think before you dash off that next aside. Would commas work as well? Or parentheses? Perhaps the sentence could be rewritten? Or split into two sentences? For those times when only dashes will do, here's how they work.

- Use a single dash as you would a colon, to introduce a piece of information. *As he stared at the equation, Werner wore his usual expression—uncertainty.*

- Use two dashes as you would parentheses, to separate an aside or an explanation from the rest of a sentence. *Enrico was a high-energy guy—he could be explosive at times—but his reactions were usually controlled.*

- Use parentheses or commas instead if you want the interruption to be less intrusive. *Marie looked radiant (even for her) as she emerged from the lab. What she liked most about Pierre, as she often told him, was his magnetic personality.*

- Use no more than two dashes per sentence, or readers won't know what's being set off from what. Clunky: *Niels's background—he came from a nuclear family—seemed appropriate for an atomic scientist—he even specialized in the nucleus.* Better:

Niels's background—he came from a nuclear fam-
ily—seemed appropriate for an atomic scientist. He
even specialized in the nucleus.

Use dashes sparingly, and the reader won't have to
be an Einstein to decipher your message.

Hyphenomena

Don't take the hyphen for granted. It can change
your meaning 180 degrees. This means one thing:
When Mr. Drysdale offered her a new contract, Miss
Hathaway reluctantly resigned. This means the oppo-
site: *When Mr. Drysdale offered her a new contract,*
Miss Hathaway reluctantly re-signed.

Still not convinced? Try this: *Jethro bought the*
chicks their own coop. Now this: *Jethro bought the chicks*
their own co-op. Or this: *Granny hoped to recover the*
stolen couch. And this: *Granny hoped to re-cover the*
stolen couch.

Hyphens become an issue when a word joins another or takes on an addition, either at the front (a
prefix) or at the back (a suffix). Some of these combos
get hyphens and some don't. Fortunately, there are
tricks to help you figure this out. Trick number one is
to go to the dictionary. If the answer isn't there, these
suggestions may help you deal with prefixes, suffixes,
and two-word combinations.

First let's look at words with prefixes (like *anti, ex,*
mini, re, and *ultra*) and suffixes (such as *less* and *like*).

- Use a hyphen to avoid confusion with another word that's spelled the same. *Granny didn't* **resent** *having her letter returned. She just added a stamp and* **re-sent** *it.*

- Use a hyphen if the combined word would be hard to read without one. *Jed wasn't* **anti-art**, *but he preferred his soup cans in the cupboard, not on the wall.*

- Use a hyphen if the original word starts with a capital letter. *Mrs. Drysdale yearned for a* **Clampett-less** *world and a* **goatless** *neighborhood.*

- Use a hyphen if the combination would create a double vowel, such as *aa, ee,* and so on. *Minnie Pearl was Granny's favorite* **anti-intellectual**. (There are some exceptions with *pre* and *re,* so check the dictionary.)

- Use a hyphen when adding *like* to a word ending in l. *Foul language had never tainted Elly May's* **shell-like** *ears.*

- Use hyphens after *ex, quasi,* and *self. Jethro's* **ex-girlfriend** *once had a* **quasi-legal** *marriage to a* **self-promoting** *rodeo star.*

  Now the two-word combinations.

- Use a hyphen if a two-word description (like *two-word*) comes before a noun (like *description*) and either part of the combination couldn't stand alone. *The Clampetts' former home was a* **one-story** *cabin.* Don't use a hyphen if both words could be used alone and still make sense. *On the porch was a **fine old** rocker.*

- Don't use a hyphen if a two-word description comes after the noun it describes. *The cabin was **one story**, not counting the oil rig in the living room.*
- Don't use a hyphen when *very* is part of a description. *Elly May was a **very accomplished** child.* (This is even true when *very* is added to a description that already has a hyphen. *She was a **much-admired** majorette. In fact, she was a **very much admired** majorette.*)
- Don't use a hyphen with *most* or *least* or *less*. If the word comes at the front of a description, keep it separate. *Granny's **most comfortable** shoes, and her **least expensive** ones, were from **less exclusive** stores.* If *most* or *less* is at the end of a description, attach it without a hyphen. *Those **heartless** clerks at Kmart put her size on the **topmost** shelf.*
- Don't use a hyphen if one of the two words is an *ly* adverb, like *busily, cleverly, mercifully, vigorously,* and so on. *Jed's bloodhound, Duke, had **feverishly erotic** dreams about the Drysdales' poodle.*
- Use a hyphen with a fraction. *The Clampetts deposited **nine-tenths** of their fortune in Mr. Drysdale's bank.*

While we're on the subject of fractions and hyphens, the word *half* is all over the place—*halfback, half gainer, half-life*—so check the dictionary for the *half*s and *half*-nots.

Apostrophic Illness

If you think all this hoo-ha about punctuation is too pedantic for words, drop in on a cheeky newsgroup called alt.possessive.its.has.no.apostrophe. Pedantry, it turns out, can be a lot of fun. Imagine the brothers Fowler in a Monty Python sketch.

We couldn't resist mentioning alt.possessive.its. has.no.apostrophe in a discussion of the least understood and most abused of punctuation marks. Pity the poor apostrophe, doomed to show up at the wrong time or the wrong place, from message board to billboard, e-mail to snail mail.

Believe it or not, there are entire Web pages devoted to apostrophe abuse, featuring screw-ups of every conceivable kind. Dunkin' Donuts, a company that ought to know better, referred in a coupon to *flavored coffee's* (make that *coffees*). An Exxon station offered a discount of four cents a gallon on *Sunday's & Monday's* (oops, *Sundays & Mondays*). A local Blockbuster said *Thank's* (no, thanks). The saddest example we found was an epitaph to a woman laid to rest as *Glady's*.

Apparently, many people think every word ending in *s* ought to have an apostrophe in there someplace. It ain't necessarily so. In fact, most words ending in *s* shouldn't have apostrophes at all.

The main job of the apostrophe is to show ownership (**Hank's** pet peeve or **Frank's** nit-picking or the **brothers'** idiosyncrasies). It also moonlights, primarily as a stand-in for missing letters (Hank and Frank **didn't** conjugate after four **o'clock**).

This is how to use (or not use) the apostrophe to show ownership.

- Add 's to any noun, singular or plural, that doesn't end in s already. "Look at this **bird's** plumage, squire," said Hank. "Makes you think of **women's** hats."
- Add only the apostrophe to a plural noun that already ends in s. "Other **parrots'** feathers are a bloody embarrassment," he added.
- Don't add an apostrophe to a pronoun that shows ownership (like *its, his, hers, ours, theirs, yours*). "Wake up, Polly Parrot," said Hank. "This cuttlefish is all **yours**."

This is how to make the apostrophe stand in for missing letters.

- Use an apostrophe to show where letters have been dropped to form a contraction (like *isn't,* short for *is not*). "Look, my lad, **I've** had just about enough of this," said Frank.
- Use an apostrophe to show where letters have been dropped from a word. "**Pinin'** for the fjords?" Frank said. "This bird is **bleedin'** demised!"

Now for a few odds 'n' endings about apostrophes.

We've said it before, but it's worth repeating. *It's* and *its* are not interchangeable. *It's* is a contraction, two words in one, while *its* is a possessive, a word showing ownership. *"It's dead,"* Frank said. *"It's rung down the curtain and gone to meet its maker."* (You can read more about *its* versus *it's* in chapter 11.)

And remember, plural words don't get apostrophes merely because they end in *s*. As for plural numbers (*6's* and *7's* or *1980's*) and letters (*p's* and *q's*), opinions differ, but we recommend adding apostrophes to make them easier to read. *"Listen," said Hank, "he's reciting his ABC's."*

Finally, when a word ends in an apostrophe, any other punctuation (like a period or a comma) follows it. *Even the King's English wasn't as good as the brothers'.*

Afterword

As we were finishing *You Send Me,* our friend Deb and her daughter, Sophie, a high school senior, stayed with us for a couple of weeks to scope out colleges in the East. Their plan was to use our place in Connecticut as a base while they made short trips to various corners of New England. This kept them busy, so they didn't mind that we were too distracted with the book to be attentive hosts.

Engineering this project was quite a feat for Deb, as you can imagine. Besides flying herself and Sophie and their accoutrements from Arizona to Connecticut, she had to make a jillion college appointments, arrange untold bed-and-breakfast stays, map driving routes, then pack Sophie off to France for a month abroad, dump the rental car, rest with us for a few days, and fly back to Phoenix. All this took weeks to plan.

Naturally, Deb did almost everything on the Internet—plane tickets, car rental, B&B reservations, maps and directions, plus her communications with us as the itinerary took shape. The final printouts filled a thick loose-leaf binder that she carried around like a Baedeker.

One day, as we were writing and our guests were traipsing through the ivy in Massachusetts, a thought struck us. How on earth could Deb have arranged this expedition without e-mail? Letters back and forth would have taken forever. (There was the time she e-mailed us a quick question about renting a car while she had the rental agency's Web site waiting in another window.) And phone calls, apart from the awkward three-hour time difference, would have been costly and inefficient. Either way, she wouldn't have had that tidy record of printouts to guide her from campus to campus, covered bridge to B&B.

Yes, she could have managed without e-mail (Kerouac did, and he was on the road for months), but the idea never crossed her mind. It wouldn't have crossed ours, either. Or yours, we'll bet.

Somehow, without our realizing it, e-mail has become indispensable. It's the way we live now. It's no longer a new way to communicate; it's *the* way to communicate. Like it or not (and sometimes we don't), there's no going back. Until some genius comes along with a better idea, writing to each other will largely mean writing online. We might as well get it right.

Bibliography

The American Heritage Dictionary of the English Language. 4th ed. Boston: Houghton Mifflin, 2000.

The Careful Writer: A Modern Guide to English Usage. Theodore M. Bernstein. New York: Free Press, 1995.

A Dictionary of Contemporary American Usage. Bergen Evans and Cornelia Evans. New York: Random House, 1957.

A Dictionary of Modern English Usage. H. W. Fowler. 2nd ed., revised by Sir Ernest Gowers. New York: Oxford University Press, 1983.

*Doublespeak Defined: Cut Through the Bull**** and Get the Point.* William Lutz. New York: Harper-Resource, 1999.

The Elements of Style. William Strunk, Jr., and E. B. White. 3rd ed. New York: Macmillan, 1979.

Essentials of English Grammar. Otto Jespersen. Tuscaloosa: University of Alabama Press, 1964.

Harper's English Grammar. John B. Opdycke. Revised ed. New York: Warner Books, 1991.

A Mathematician Reads the Newspaper. John Allen Paulos. New York: Anchor Books, 1996.

The New York Public Library Writer's Guide to Style and Usage. New York: HarperCollins, 1994.

The New York Times Manual of Style and Usage. Revised ed. Allan M. Siegal and William G. Connolly. New York: Three Rivers Press, 2001.

On Writing Well: An Informal Guide to Writing Non-fiction. William Zinsser. 6th ed. New York: Harper-Perennial, 1998.

The Oxford Dictionary of American Usage and Style. Bryan A. Garner. New York: Oxford University Press, 2000.

Plain Words: Their ABC. Sir Ernest Gowers. New York: Knopf, 1968.

The Psychology of the Internet. Patricia Wallace. New York: Cambridge University Press, 2001.

The Reader over Your Shoulder: A Handbook for Writers of English Prose. Robert Graves and Alan Hodge. New York: Macmillan, 1943.

Simple & Direct: A Rhetoric for Writers. Jacques Barzun. Revised ed. Chicago: University of Chicago Press, 1994.

Style: Toward Clarity and Grace. Joseph M. Williams. Chicago: University of Chicago Press, 1995.

Webster's New World College Dictionary. 4th ed. New York: John Wiley & Sons, 1999.

Woe Is I: The Grammarphobe's Guide to Better English in Plain English. Patricia T. O'Conner. New York: Riverhead, 1998.

Words Fail Me: What Everyone Who Writes Should Know About Writing. Patricia T. O'Conner. San Diego: Harvest, 1999.

Index

abbreviations
  e-mail shorthand and,
    14, 43, 50–51,
    67–69, 140, 144
  periods and, 203–4
-able/-ible, 189
absolute terms, 131–32
acronyms. *see*
  abbreviations
active voice, 116–18
address, e-mail
  accuracy of, 23
  hiding, 38-40, 143
  parts of, 31-33
  shared, 36
address book, 39, 145
adjectives, 119–20
adverbs, 119
affect/effect, 173
aggravate/irritate, 174
all, 157
all ready/already, 178
all right, 178

all together/altogether, 178
along with, 156
American Management
  Association, 19
among/between, 174
anger
  e-mail and, 11, 12–13,
    145
  flame wars and, 59–61
Animal Farm (novel), 110
Anna Karenina (novel),
  215
anonymity, 12, 63, 79–80
answering machine,
  69–70, 103
any, 157
any more/anymore, 178
any one/anyone, 178–79
any time/anytime, 179
any way/anyway, 179
AOL, 33, 71, 187
apostrophes, 159–60, 201,
  222–24

arithmetic mean, 139
as/like, 166–67
as well as, 156
asides, pointy brackets
    and, 14, 66–67
Ask Jeeves, 86
attachments, e-mail, 22,
    41–42, 53, 56, 144
Austen, Jane, 95
average, 139

bad/badly, 174
between/among, 174
big words, 108
blind copies, 38–40, 143
Blockbuster, 222
Blondell, Joan, 82
-body, 168–69
body language, 54
bread-and-butter notes,
    51–52
bring/take, 174
bulletin boards, 4, 9, 21
    anonymity and, 79–80
    lurking on, 76–77
    posting to, 70–71
    separate screen name
        for, 28, 57
bureaucratic language, 108

can/may, 174
capitalization
    after colons, 212
    importance of, 24, 144
    shouting, 23–24

Carnegie, Dale, 13
Carnivore, 21
Case, Steve, 187
Catch-22 (novel), 110
CBS, 78
-cede/-ceed/-sede, 191
chain letters, 10, 56, 85–86
chat rooms, 3–4, 9, 10, 28
    anonymity and, 79–80
    lurking in, 76–77
    posting to, 71–74
    private, 73–74
    separate screen name
        for, 28, 57
cheating, 89–91
clarity, 111–13, 142
clauses, 207, 208, 213
clichés, 121–28
closings, 12, 14, 42–44,
    143
colons, 211–12, 216, 218
color, 77–78
colorful words, 118–20
combined words, 220–21
commas, 203, 205–8,
    212, 216, 218
communities, virtual, 9,
    28, 60
compliments, 48–49
conferences, virtual
    business, 62
confidentiality, surveillance
    of e-mail, 19–23
confused words, 172–81
conjunctions, 170

connecting words/phrases, 111–12
contractions, 135, 170, 223
contradictions, 130–31
convince/persuade, 174–75
cooling-off period, 11, 12–13, 145
copying, excessive, 38–39, 41, 56, 101, 142, 145
courtesy notes, 51–53
criticism, 48, 60–61

dashes, 204, 208, 217–19
data, 176
David Copperfield (novel), 214,
decimated, 175
descriptive words/phrases, 115
Desk Set (movie), 82–83
Dialectizer, 77
dictionaries, 145–46, 183–84
dilemma, 175
discussion groups
    flames in, 59–61
    sales pitches and, 58
    separate screen name for, 28, 57
disinterested/uninterested, 175
disorderly writing, 113–15
domain names, 33
double negatives, 171
Dow Chemical, 19

downloads
    red flags at work, 22
    unsuitable attachments, 41–42, 53, 56
    viruses and, 35, 41, 42
Dunkin' Donuts, 222

e-mail
    addiction, 47–48
    alternatives to, 46–49, 51–55, 145
    anger and, 11, 12–13, 59–61, 145
    avoidance, 47
    compared with a phone call, 5, 28, 29–31
    complaints about, 9–10
    curtness and, 9–15, 30, 140, 143
    customizing, 77–78
    dos and don'ts, 140–46
    indiscreet, 19–23, 143
    length of, 36–37, 100–103, 141–42
    organizing the message, 36–37
    overload, 55–56, 95–96
    personal versus business, 15–16
    quality of writing and, 3–4, 5, 30-31
    red flags in, 22–23
    replying to, 15–18, 25–26, 29–30, 33–34, 37–38, 142–43

e-mail (*continued*)
  sorting, 16–17, 35,
    101–2
  stress caused by, 9–10, 46
  surveillance of, 19–23
  techno-clutter, 38, 56
e-rater, 105
e-zines, 74–76
Educational Testing
  Service, 105–6
effect/affect, 173
e.g./i.e., 175
either . . . or, 157
ellipses, 205
emigrate/immigrate, 175
Emma (novel), 110
emoticons, 14, 50–51,
  65–67, 140, 144,
  201–2, 213, 215
employee evaluation, 48
empty openings, 97–100
Encyclopaedia Britannica,
  88
Eudora, 13
euphemisms, 109
every day/everyday, 179
every one/everyone, 179
exclamation points, 204,
  208–9, 210, 215,
  216
Exxon, 222

face time, 54–55
facial expression, 54
fad expressions, 172–73

FAQ (frequently asked
  questions), 76–77
favors, 26, 48, 58
FBI, 21
fewer/less, 176
*Fifteen Thousand Useful
  Phrases* (book), 97
figuratively, 180
flames, 59–61, 76
flaunt/flout, 176
foreign terms, 109
fortuitous, 176
forwarding, 40–41,
  49–50, 85–86, 142
fractions, 221
-ful, 198–99
fulsome, 176–77

gambling, 20, 22
games, 22
gantlet/gauntlet, 177
Gates, Bill, 20, 167–68,
  187
geniuspapers.com, 90
Gettysburg Address,
  103–4
Gibson, Mel, 87
Gone With the Wind
  (novel), 215
good/well, 177
Google, 149
gossip, 48, 143
graduate, 177
Graduate Management
  Admission Test, 105–6

grammar, 3, 4, 6, 30, 76, 140, 145–46, 149–71
grammar-checkers, 145–46, 167–68, 187
graphics, splashy, 24–25
Greenspan, Alan, 111
greeting cards, 41, 51–53
greetings. *see* salutations

hackers, 21, 198
half-, 221–22
Hammett, Dashiell, 89
harassment, 22
Hepburn, Katharine, 82
Help! (movie), 204
hero, 177–79
historic/historical, 179
home pages. *see* Web pages
homework, cheating on, 89–91
honesty, 78–79
hopefully, 180
Hotmail, 31
Howards End (novel), 183
Huckleberry Finn (novel), 110
humor, 10, 49–51, 79, 140, 144
hyphens, 219–22

i before *e* (rule), 185
I/me, 151–52
-ible/able, 189
-icky, 190
idiomatic expressions, 133

i.e./e.g., 175
if . . . were/was, 163–64
illogical writing, 129–39
images, nonsensical, 133–34
immigrate/emigrate, 175
imply/infer, 180
in addition to, 156
information overload, 95
instant messages, 3–4, 9, 10, 61–62
Internet addiction, 47–48
Internet myths, 87
Internet searches, 88–89
intimacy, avoiding, 28
irony, 79
irony, 180
irritate/aggravate, 174
it, 112
its/it's, 150, 153, 224

jargon, 106–7, 108, 140, 144
job hunting, 22
jokes, 10, 49–51, 140, 144
junk mail. *see* spam

Kierkegaard, Soren, 44
Kissinger, Henry, 155

lay/lie, 161–62
lazystudents.com, 90
less/fewer, 176
letters (of the alphabet), plurals of, 159

letters (snail mail), 46–49, 53, 54, 84, 145
libel, 21
lie/lay, 161–62
like/as, 166–67
literally, 180
lowercase letters, 24, 144
lurking, 76–77
-ly, 221

mailing lists
  lurking on, 76–77
  posting to, 70–71
  sales pitches and, 58
majority, 156–57
manners, 9-15, 143
mass mailings, 11, 58–59, 145
may/can, 174
may/might, 161
me/I, 151–52
mean, 139
meaningless words and phrases, 120
media, 176
median, 139
meetings, face-to-face, 54–55
Merrill, Dina, 82
Microsoft, 62, 167, 187
might/may, 161
Miltie, Uncle, 183
Milton, John, 183
minimalism, 103–4

misinformation, 10, 78–79, 81–91, 142
  credibility and, 82–84, 86–89
  forwarded messages, 85–86
  plagiarism and, 89–91
  speed versus accuracy, 81–82, 84
Monroe, Marilyn, 87
Monty Python, 222
most/least/less, 221
Mrs. Dalloway (novel), 90, 110
multiplication, 138
music downloads, 22, 41

names, plurals of, 158–59
nauseated/nauseous, 180–81
negatives, 134–36, 171
Neiman Marcus, 40
neither . . . nor, 157
Netspeak, 77
New York Times, The, 19, 74
newsgroups, 28
  anonymity and, 79–80
  lurking on, 76–77
  posting to, 70–71
  separate screen name for, 28, 57
none, 157, 170–71
nonsense expressions, 133–34

not, 134–36
nouns
    adjectives with, 119–20
    verbs versus, 118–19
    weak, 119–120
number, 156–57
numbers, 136–39, 142
    plurals of, 159

oversized words, 108
Owens, David, 140
oxymorons, 133

Palliser, Plantagenet, 89
paragraphs, short, 24, 111, 144
parentheses, 204, 205, 208, 209, 211, 214–15, 216–17, 218
Pascal, Blaise, 100
passive voice, 116–18
patience, 14
percentages, 138
periods, 203–5, 216
persuade/convince, 174–75
PGP (Pretty Good Privacy), 21
place, being clear about, 112–13
plagiarism, 89–91
platitudes, 124–28
plurals, 157–59, 176, 223, 224
politeness, 9–15, 143

porn, 22
possessives, 153, 159–60, 223, 224
Power and the Glory, The (novel), 110
PowerPoint, 103–4
praise, 48
prefixes, 219–20
prepositions, at end of sentence, 170
Pride and Prejudice (novel), 95
privacy
    screen name and, 21–22, 28, 57
    surveillance of e-mail, 19–23
promotional methods, 58–59
promotions, employee requests for, 48
proportions, 138–39
prurient messages, 27–28
pseudoscientific terms, 109–10
punctuation, 24, 30, 31, 145–46, 201–24

question marks, 204, 209–11, 215, 216
quotation marks, 205, 207, 209, 215–17
quoting e-mail, 38, 40-41, 56, 101, 142

racism, 22
rack/wrack, 181
raises, requests for, 48
redundancy, 102
rejection, in e-mail,
    25–26, 28
Reply All, 38–40
rereading, importance of,
    11, 30, 129–30, 145,
    184
resignation notices, 48
respecting the reader, 64,
    75–76
romance, 27–28, 143
rudeness, 9-15
rumors, 48, 143

-s/-es/-ies, 158
-s/-'s, 153, 159–60, 223
salutations, 12, 14,
    42–44, 143
Schroeder, Pat, 79
screen names
    information in, 31–33
    privacy and, 21–22
    shared, 36
    using separate, 21–22,
        28, 57
search engines, 86–89, 149
security breaches, 22
Select All, 38
-self, 152–53
semicolons, 212–14, 216
Send Later, 11
sensitive subjects, 79

sentences, short, 111
series
    colon with, 212
    commas with, 207
    semicolons with,
        213–14
sexism, 22, 27–28
shouting, 23–24
signatures, 12, 14, 42–44,
    143
    tag lines with, 44–45,
        215
*Sir Harry Hotspur of
    Humblethwaite*
    (novel), 89
smileys. *see* emoticons
sorting e-mail, 16–17, 35,
    101–2
spam, 10, 56–59, 144–45
    deleting, 34–35
    screen names and, 31
    subject lines and, 34,
        144–45
special effects, unintended,
    131
spelling, 3, 4, 5, 30,
    145–46, 182–200
    "creative," 24–25,
        182–83, 198
    dictionaries and,
        145–46, 183–84
    problem words,
        184–200
    rereading and, 30,
        129–30, 145, 184

spell-checkers and, 6,
140, 146, 184,
186–87
split infinitives, 170, 171
spying on employees,
19–23
stationary/stationery, 181
Stern, Howard, 183
stress, 9–10
subject
agreement with verb,
155–57
location of verb and,
114–15
subject lines, 12, 18–19,
33–36, 141
hype in, 58
for important messages,
18–19, 35
replying and, 38
spam and, 34,
144–45
suffixes, 219–20
superlatives, 131–32
surveillance of e-mail,
19–23
sympathy notes, 52–53

tact-checking, 10–13
tag lines, 44–45, 215
take/bring, 174
technical language, 108,
142
techno-clutter, 38, 56
telegramese, 67–69

telephone, 4, 28, 29–31,
46–49, 54–55,
70–71, 145
tense, 160–61
termination of employees,
19
than/then, 181
that/which, 165–66
their/there/they're, 150,
162–63
then/than, 181
there/they're/their, 150,
162–63
they/them/their, 169
they're/their/there, 150,
162–63
Thin Man, The (novel), 89
time, being clear about,
112–13
together with, 156
tone of voice, 54
tone of writing, 11, 14
total, 156–57
Tracy, Spencer, 82
trendy words, 108
triteness, 121–28
Trollope, Anthony, 89
truth, stretching, 78–79
typography, 24–25, 76,
77–78

unclear writing, 111–15,
129–39
uninterested/disinterested,
175

unique, 181
United Press International,
    67–68
uppercase letters, 23–24,
    144
urban legends, 87
user names. *see* screen
    names

verbs
    active voice and, 116–18
    adverbs with, 119
    agreement with subject,
        155–57
    location of subject and,
        114–15
    nouns versus, 118–19
    split infinitives, 170,
        171
    strong versus weak, 119
    tense of, 160–61
very/much, 221
Victoria's Secret, 85–86
viruses, 35, 41, 42
vocabulary, 64, 105, 118,
    142
voice mail, 62, 69–70
vulgarity, 22

Web pages, 3–4, 9, 10,
    21, 74–76
Web publications, 74–76
Web surfing, 22
well/good, 177

"When You Are Old"
    (poem), 110
which/that, 165–66
who/whom, 154–55
who's/whose, 164–65
*Why Do Clocks Run
    Clockwise?* (book), 204
will/would, 161
Wodehouse, P. G., 88
Woolf, Virginia, 90
wordiness, 102
would/will, 161
wrack/rack, 181
writing online
    customizing for
        audience, 63–80
    dos and don'ts, 140–146
    ease of, 4, 96
    problems of, 10, 11–12,
        31, 95
    quality of, 3–6, 10,
        30–31, 74–76, 80,
        149-51
    warm-up exercises,
        13–14
    for Web publications,
        74–76

X-rated e-mail, 22, 27–28
Xerox, 19

Yeats, William Butler, 110
your/you're, 150, 163